OUR HANDS ARE STAINED WITH BLOOD

THE TRAGIC STORY OF THE "CHURCH" AND THE JEWISH PEOPLE

Other Books by Michael L. Brown

From Holy Laughter to Holy Fire:
America on the Edge of Revival

Israel's Divine Healer
(Studies in Old Testament Biblical Theology)

It's Time to Rock the Boat:
A Call to God's People to Rise Up and
Preach a Confrontational Gospel

Whatever Happened to the Power of God:
Is the Charismatic Church Slain in the Spirit
or Down for the Count?

How Saved Are We?

The End of the American Gospel Enterprise

Compassionate Father or Consuming Fire?
Who Is the God of the Old Testament?

Let No One Deceive You:
Confronting the Critics of Revival

For information on ICN Ministries, or for a listing of other books and tapes by Michael L. Brown, write to:

ICN Ministries
P.O. Box 36157
Pensacola, FL 32506
Phone: (850) 458-6424
FAX: (850) 458-1828
E-mail: RevivalNow@msn.com

OUR HANDS ARE STAINED WITH BLOOD

THE TRAGIC STORY OF THE "CHURCH" AND THE JEWISH PEOPLE

BY
MICHAEL L. BROWN

Destiny Image® Publishers, Inc.
P.O. Box 310
Shippensburg, PA 17257-0310

"Speaking to the Purposes of God for This Generation
and for the Generations to Come"

ISBN 1-56043-068-0

For Worldwide Distribution
Printed in the U.S.A.

Fifth Printing: 1996   Sixth Printing: 1997

This book and all other Destiny Image, Revival Press,
and Treasure House books are available
at Christian bookstores and distributors worldwide.

For a U.S. bookstore nearest you, call **1-800-722-6774**.
For more information on foreign distributors,
call **717-532-3040**.
Or reach us on the Internet: **http://www.reapernet.com**

Contents

Foreword

It is said of a good book, "I could not put it down." I must say of *Our Hands Are Stained With Blood,* "I wanted to put it down, set it aside, not read it or deal with its issues"—but I couldn't. The Lord would not let me put it down. I was too convicted. Convicted of my ignorance. Ignorance of the spirit of anti-Semitism that has been in the Church and in many so-called Christians throughout history. I did not know the extent of persecution by Gentile "Christians" toward our Jewish brethren in the past. I know it now—thanks to Mike Brown's thorough research and indisputable historical facts. The statements of Christian leaders of the past toward the Jew left me shaken and awakened.

What scares me is that a similar spirit of anti-Semitism is in the Church today among some segments of the Body of Christ. This has come in the form of a popular teaching circulating in the Church today called "Replacement Theology," the idea that the Church is the new Israel, and that the Church alone is the fulfillment of the Old Testament prophecies regarding God's covenant with the Jewish people. If you have struggled with this question out of either ignorance or personal conviction, I challenge you to read chapters 12 and 13 of this book prayerfully. Mike's interpretation of the apostle Paul's teaching on who is Israel and who is a Jew is indisputable. To any sincere student of the Word these chapters will forever establish in your mind and heart that we Christians are *not* the new Jew or true Jew, that God has not and never will forsake His people, and that the possession of the Land by Israel is a right not granted by man but miraculously promised by God in perpetuity.

This book is therefore a wake-up call to the Church. As a pastor I want all anti-Semitism to stop at the church door. It must have no place among true Christians. Wherever we see this attitude raise its ugly head we must work to change it. And may intercessors be raised up to pray for the gospel to go "to the Jew first."

I consider myself to be a lover of Israel and of the Jewish people. But there were blind spots in my vision toward the Jews. Mike Brown's message made me, I believe, better prepared to pray for and work toward the peace of Jerusalem.

My prayer is that you will be as deeply moved as I was by this book, and that you will see that it gets in the hands of pastors, Christian leaders and laymen, as I plan to do— whether they are sensitive to Jewish issues or not. No one can be the same toward the Jewish people, both those who believe in Jesus and those who do not, after reading *Our Hands Are Stained With Blood.*

Don Wilkerson
Times Square Church

Publisher's Foreword

This book needed to be written. Gentile believers need to know what was done to the Jewish people over the centuries in the name of Jesus.

We Gentile believers need to understand the pain and suffering that countless pseudo-Christians have brought upon the Jewish people. Only then can we even begin to comprehend the depth of the pain and sorrow they have endured at the hands of so-called "Christians".

Although much of what you will read cannot be attributed to genuine Christian believers, some of it can. There is an unnerving trend toward a renewed anti-Semitic spirit, even among Christians, not only in the United States, but worldwide.

We need to understand our responsibility "to stand in the gap" on behalf of God's still-chosen people. Genuine prayers of intercession need to be offered on the behalf of Israel. Heart prayers of repentance need to be offered on behalf of those genuine Christian brethren who have carried and still do carry such hate in their hearts. Resolve must be born deep in our spirits that will expose anti-Semitic attitudes both in ourselves and those around us.

Finally, we need to be reminded to pray for the peace of Jerusalem, as the Scripture commands us to do, that the glory of the Lord might subdue the earth, and that at His coming, there would be a Bride made up of Jewish and Gentile believers alike, standing together in genuine unity and in the bonds of peace.

Preface
(How to Read this Book)

In a speech delivered in 1985, Richard Von Weizsaecker, the President of Germany, made these important remarks:

> *The Jewish nation remembers and will always remember.* We seek reconciliation. Precisely for this reason we must understand that *there can be no reconciliation without remembrance.* The experience of millionfold death is part of the very being of every Jew in the world, not only because people cannot forget such atrocities, but also because *remembrance is part of the Jewish faith.*[1]

Yes, "remembrance is part of the Jewish faith." Over and over, God commanded His people Israel to remember and never forget:

> *Remember* the day you stood before the Lord at Horeb...
> *Remember* that you were slaves in Egypt and that the Lord your God brought you out of there with a mighty hand and an outstretched arm....

Remember well what the Lord your God did to Pharaoh and to all Egypt....
Remember how the Lord your God led you all the way in the desert these forty years...
Remember this and *never forget* how you provoked the Lord your God to anger in the desert....
Remember what the Lord your God did to Miriam along the way after you came out of Egypt....
Remember what the Amalekites did to you along the way when you came out of Egypt....
Do not forget![2]

This is a lesson we Jews have learned well: Our painful history is indelibly inscribed in our souls. But there are others who cannot remember because they have never known. In the words of the Catholic scholar Edward Flannery:

> The vast majority of Christians, even well educated, are all but totally ignorant of what happened to Jews in history and of the culpable involvement of the Church....*It is little exaggeration to state that those pages of history Jews have committed to memory are the very ones that have been torn from Christian (and secular) history books.*[3]

How tragic that *Christians*—a people redeemed by a Jewish Messiah and instructed by Jewish apostles, joint heirs of Israel's Scriptures and grafted into Israel's olive tree—should be almost totally ignorant of two thousand years of Jewish agony. Over the last few years, as I have read and re-read the excruciating chapters of my Jewish people's past, sometimes falling asleep at night sobbing, shaken and stunned, God has stirred my heart with a burning message: The Church must know!

But that is only the beginning. It is the Christian Church—in name, though not in spirit—that has actually written much of Israel's unbearably painful history, using Jewish blood instead of ink. To this day, the name "Jesus Christ" is considered a swear word in many Jewish homes. The Savior's precious name has become profanity, tarnished by the evils done in His name by those who call themselves His people. It is time we Christians become aware of this shameful past so that there might be a glorious future—for Israel and the Church.

At times, as you read this book, you will want to stop and put it down. The story is too painful. *But it is a story that must be taken to heart.* For the only way that these sins against the Jewish people will ever be blotted out, the only way that we will ever see a truly international revival, the only way that we will ever be ministers of God's grace to Israel, is if we fully acknowledge the guilt and shame of our "Christian" ancestors, and with anguished heart, repent. Whether Catholic or Protestant—there is blood on our fathers' hands.

But is there blood on *our* hands too? Are true believers today responsible for the sins of those who claimed to be believers in past generations? In what sense is there blood on the hands of the *true Church*? These are important questions!

It is a tragic fact of history that the *outward, visible* Church is stained with the blood of the Jewish people. This painful memory is so vivid in Jewish hearts that an Orthodox Jewish author, in a book published in *1991*, could say: "Today, one of the most fundamental causes of Jewish suffering is the hatred of Christians towards Jews and the Jewish faith."

This Jewish author actually believes:

From his birth, every Christian, practicing or nominal, imbibes the belief that the Jews, i.e., any and every individual Jew, are answerable for the murder of his messiah. Indeed, the overwhelming majority of the acts of persecution, religious coercion and massacres suffered in history by our People came at the hands of the Christians. Thus we see that Christianity was a significant and major cause of Jewish suffering (Meir Simcha Sokolovsky).[4]

As you read some of the chapters that follow—especially as you realize that for many Jews, this "Christianity" was the only brand they ever saw—you will feel revulsion, shock and anger. No doubt your reaction will be, "But that's not the real Church! That's not me! True Christians are filled with love, not hate."

On the one hand, that is absolutely true. The Church that butchered Jewish men, women and children could only be a thoroughly apostate Church. In order to emphasize that point, I have often put the words "Church" and "Christian" in quotation marks. Throughout the book, you will be reminded of that.

But it is not just the apostate Church that has sinned. The wrong theology—and even arrogance—of many leaders within the *true Church* helped pave the way for the full-blown, violent "Christian" anti-Semitism that you will be reading about. The true Church must take responsibility too! It is for this reason also that I have sometimes put the words "Church" and "Christian" in quotation marks. The attitudes and actions of many within the true Church at times have hardly been "Christian"!

During times of great Jewish suffering, right up to this century, much of the Church has remained indifferent to the Jewish people's pain. For this sin too, we must take blame. And there are the seeds of anti-Semitism that fester among believers today. For all these things, we must repent.

I am convinced that international Christian repentance for the Church's past (and present) sins against the Jews will lead to international Jewish repentance for Israel's past (and present) sins against Jesus. *It is the Church's tears of repentance that will wash away the stain of blood.*

You might ask, "But how can I *repent*? I love Israel and the Jewish people."

First, you can give yourself to *intercessory repentance* by recognizing, renouncing and feeling grief for the anti-Semitism of the "Church." The prophets of Israel repented of the sins of their nation, saying, "WE have sinned"— even though they themselves may not have been guilty. But as the spiritual remnant, they took intercessory responsibility for the carnal majority, and on behalf of those who had sinned, repented. You can do the same today!

Second, you can search your own heart to see if there is any seed of anti-Semitism within you. Do you lack compassion for the Jewish people in their suffering, thinking to yourself, "Well, they're only getting what they deserve!" (As if all Jewish suffering has been caused by the words spoken by the crowd in Matthew 27:25—"His blood [i.e., Jesus' blood] be on us and on our children!")

Have you been asleep while the Jews have been slaughtered? Are you indifferent to the satanic world conspiracy against Israel? If you are not Jewish, do you somehow feel threatened by the fact that the Jews are still chosen and loved? Questions like these must be asked honestly. There may be more pollution within us than we would like to acknowledge!

Third, we must realize that both in the past and in the present, the erroneous theology of *true Christians* has helped open the door for all types of murderous persecutions of the Jews. The fact that some of this theology is still alive today is strong evidence that the contemporary Church needs to repent.

With a great sense of urgency, and with the perspective of one who calls both Jews and believing Christians "my people" (in other words, as a Jewish follower of Jesus), I send this book forth. That I send it forth with such urgency is easily explained. *Even now, the enemies of Israel are many, but its friends are few.*

Although it is difficult to comprehend, America has dealt with men like Syria's Hafez Assad—committed to Israel's annihilation, and armed to the teeth with sophisticated weaponry—as if they were trusted friends. Every day, international pressure mounts against the Jewish state.

Although it hardly seems possible, neo-Nazi computer games are sweeping through Europe, rewarding the young players who can torture and kill the most Jews with promotions to more powerful positions in this death-camp video madness. One Austrian teenager remarked, "Gassing Jews is terrific!" These games have now made their way into Canada.

Although it sounds more like a nightmare than reality, enraged mobs of young New York Blacks staged anti-Jewish riots in September of 1991, screaming, "Heil Hitler! Kill the dirty Jews!" They looted Jewish stores, vandalized Jewish schools, ransacked Jewish synagogues—and even killed a Jewish student, wounding several others as well.[5]

And while all these atrocities have been taking place, Christian leaders have been telling their flocks that God is through with Israel as a people and nation. How perverse! Worse still—this is almost beyond comprehension—there are Christian leaders whose ministries are largely devoted to warning believers to beware of evil Israel. I am not exaggerating![6]

There is still an ugly spirit in the Body that must be exposed. It is bad enough that the same diabolical spirit of anti-Semitism influences much of the world today. But that it still exists in the Church is unthinkable! Would to God that this generation of believers would finally drive out that foul spirit.

This book has been written with a burning (and often broken) heart, in the hope that the people of God *today* would utterly repudiate the Church's sins of yesterday. This will bring reconciliation—reconciliation of the Church to the Jewish people, and reconciliation of the Jewish people to their Messiah.

No doubt there will be controversy, from both Christian and Jewish perspectives.[7] I only ask that you, the reader, read this book with an open heart before God. The results are in His hands. May your heart be stirred to action as you read the pages that follow!

* * *

Some important acknowledgements are in order:

My heartfelt thanks to Chuck Cohen, a dear friend from Times Square Church in New York, who urged me in December of 1990 to pray about finishing this book. At that time I had written only a few chapters—actually I was *compelled* to write Chapter One—and I was not going to touch this work for a year or more. But Chuck sensed the importance of getting the manuscript completed, as well as the spiritual connection between Times Square Church and the message of this book. The Lord confirmed that he was right.

To Pastors Don and David Wilkerson, I express my deep appreciation for being true friends of the Jewish people, and for standing with me in the publication of this book. I am honored by Pastor Don's pointed and honest foreword.

I owe a debt of love to the devoted Christian brothers and sisters in Korea who pray fervently for the salvation and well being of Israel. Each of my trips to Korea has been marked by providential signs that God has raised up the

Korean Church to intercede for the Jewish people. It was with the help of a mighty wave of Korean intercession that most of this book was written during a three week period in January of 1991. (The endnotes were written in July and August of 1991.) During a visit to Seoul in October of 1991, the manuscript of this book was almost literally soaked in tears as we prayed and wept together. Yes, the fervent, brokenhearted praying of these Korean Christians will one day help to bring everlasting joy to my Jewish people.

I also want to acknowledge my indebtedness to my old friend Rabbi William Berman, a man who encouraged me (*provoked* me would probably be more accurate!) to learn Hebrew as a brand new believer twenty years ago. It was he who gave me my first book to read on the ugly history of "Christian" anti-Semitism. Although he does not agree with some of the contents of *this* book, I hope he will hear my heart—and the heart of our Redeemer.

Leonard and Martha Ravenhill continue to humble me with their faithful and loving prayer support (how can I express my thanks?), Mike Murray once again provided a thoughtful reading of the manuscript and Steve Homcy, my colleague here at Messiah Biblical Institute, provided me with his careful insights. Lori Smith added tears of travail and Don Nori, president of Destiny Image, helped me immeasurably by enabling me to hear the heart of a Christian man who deeply loves the Jewish people. I pray that God would reward him abundantly for standing behind this work.

My dear wife Nancy, together with our precious daughters Jennifer and Megan, give me three more eternal reasons to always please the Lord. May He be glorified through this work.

Michael L. Brown

March, 1992 (The five hundredth anniversary of the edict to expel all unbaptized Jews from Spain.)

To the reader: Don't neglect the endnotes! If you find endnotes distracting, I would suggest that you first read each chapter without the notes, and then read it again, looking up each reference. Many of the notes contain important quotations, illustrations and facts not found in the main body of the text. For those wishing to do further study, a bibliographical supplement is provided.

Chapter One

The Final Solution

You are about to go on a journey. The soldiers have ordered you aboard and the train is ready to leave. You stand side by side with your family, wondering what will come next. You are crowded into a railway cattle car, packed with dozens of other adults and children. *Where are they taking us now?*

Suddenly the doors slam shut. There is no light. There is no food. There is no water. There is very little air. You are crammed together like so many cows. And hour after hour the train rattles on; *four endless days and four endless nights.* Your younger sister stands pressed against you, clutching her baby boy in her arms. After three days her labored breathing turns to suffocated gasps. Soon she is a corpse.

Your children are moaning. Your spouse is half-crazed. Hunger and thirst rage and burn. *When will the nightmare end?* But this is only the beginning. You are soon to arrive at your destination: a Nazi extermination camp. The only way out is death. To live is a fate worse than that. How can this possibly be? Just six months ago life was so normal....

Now the doors swing open. Soldiers bark commands. They yell at you, they punch and kick. Your sister's stiff body falls to the ground. *At least the baby is still alive.* Not for long! The little boy is carefully picked up by an officer...and smashed against the wall.

Then two lines are formed, and everyone is divided. A child calls out for his frail grandmother. A husband tries to stay near his terrified wife. Your eyes dart. Your heart pounds. There is nothing you can do.

The healthy are herded to the line to the right. You are among the strong. But look once more at your family on the left. Remember your old father's eyes. Don't forget your three-year old's smile. You will never see them again. Soon a bullet will pierce the back of their necks and, dead or still alive, they will burn. Human beings massacred and thrown into a huge, flaming ditch!

But you cannot know all this now. For those on the left, it will be over in a minute. For you, the living, the ordeal has just begun. Welcome to Auschwitz, my friend.

Everywhere you see signs: *Arbeit Macht Frei,* "Work Makes Free." What can it possibly mean? But there is no time to think. Before you know it you are herded into an unheated room with others of your own sex. And you— along with everyone else—must strip. "Please, can we have something to drink?" "Tomorrow!" comes the reply.

Then a transformation takes place. You are no longer a name, but a number. Your hair is shaved off—all of it! You receive your new identity: a number tattooed on your arm. You are handed a new wardrobe comprised of assorted ill-fitting clothes. *I wonder what poor souls wore these before?* Whoever they were, they are no more. They will never need their clothes again.

Your mind is spinning. You want to wake up. You want to get out of the nightmare. But it is no dream. What is happening to you has already happened to millions of others just like you. After all, this is the Holocaust. Would you ever believe this could have taken place? Can you believe it is taking place now? *I'm freezing. I'm dying of thirst. I'm scared. Please, this can't be true.*

But this is your home for the winter. Is it possible even to survive? What does all this mean? Let another prisoner fill you in:

> It means that in the course of these months, from October to April, seven out of ten of us will die. Whoever does not die will suffer minute by minute, all day, every day: from the morning before dawn until the distribution of the evening soup we will have to keep our muscles continually tensed, dance from foot to foot, beat our arms under our shoulders against the cold. We will have to spend bread to acquire gloves, and lose hours of sleep to repair them when they become unstitched. As it will no longer be possible to eat in the open, we have to eat our meals in the hut, on our feet, everyone will be assigned an area of floor as large as a hand, as it is forbidden to rest against the bunks. Wounds will open on everyone's hands, and to be given a bandage will mean

waiting every evening for hours on one's feet [wearing shoes that always cause pain] in the snow and wind.[1]

That first night you can't sleep at all. Your body is racked. Your brain is reeling. Your bed is small for even one, but there are two of you laying on the mat. *Whose feet keep knocking against my head?* And you keep on seeing those two lines. What were they all about? Why were you chosen to go to the right while the others—the old, the sick, the babes—were sent to the left? A doctor who survived Auschwitz left this report:

> He whose destiny had directed him into the left-hand column was transformed by the gas chambers into a corpse within an hour after his arrival. [If the gas chambers and crematoriums were full, he would be shot and burned in the pyre.] Less fortunate was he whom adversity had singled out for the right-hand column. He was still a candidate for death, but with this difference, that for three or four months, or as long as he could endure, he had to submit to all the horrors the [concentration camp] had to offer, till he dropped from utter exhaustion. He bled from a thousand wounds. His belly was contorted with hunger, his eyes were haggard, and he moaned like one demented. He dragged his body across the fields of snow till he could go no farther. Trained dogs snapped at his wretched, fleshless frame, and when even the lice forsook his desiccated body, then the hour of deliverance, the hour of redeeming death was close at hand. Who then—of our parents, brothers, children—was more fortunate, he who went to the left or he who went to the right?[2]

You have been chosen to go to the right, consigned to living death. In just a few hours it will be time to rise, to stand and shiver from 3:00 A.M. until 7:00 A.M., to be counted and recounted again and again. And then, to work...for weeks and months, until you simply cannot work any more. Then it will be time for your "shower." But instead of water drenching your emaciated frame, poison gas will enter your lungs. A few hours later, your ashes will ascend to the sky through the bellowing chimneys of the death factory.

Your crime? *You are a Jew.*

And if you had a thousand lives to live, you could never fully tell how you felt that first Christmas Eve, when you lay there, a despised and worthless prisoner, and heard the prison guards, those cruel, demented guards, singing hymns and Christmas Carols....

The Church has blood on her hands.

Chapter Two
A Terrible, Tragic Past

Christianity did not create the Holocaust; indeed Nazism was anti-Christian, but it made it possible. Without Christian antisemitism, the Holocaust would have been inconceivable....Hitler and the Nazis found in medieval Catholic anti-Jewish legislation a model for their own, and they read and reprinted Martin Luther's virulently antisemitic writings. It is instructive that the Holocaust was unleashed by the only major country in Europe having approximately equal numbers of Catholics and Protestants. *Both traditions were saturated with Jew-hatred.*[1]

For nearly two thousand years...the Christian world relentlessly dehumanized the Jew, enabling the Holocaust, the ultimate consequence of this dehumanization, to take place. While it is true that many Nazis were anti-Christian (and that Nazism itself was anti-Christian), they were all, as the Jewish philosopher Eliezer Berkovitz has pointed out, the children of Christians.[2]

Christians? The children of Christians? The Christian world? How could this be? Of course, we could say that if these people were *true* Christians, if they had really been born again, they would never have done such fiendish things. And there is certainly truth to this. But it's not so simple. Some church leaders who seemed to be so "Christian," so Christlike in word and deed, also had one great, glaring weakness: They viciously maligned the Jewish people! Sometimes they even approved of violence against them. Those who claimed to be the Lord's brothers and sisters after the spirit attacked His brothers and sisters after the flesh. And this tragic story isn't over yet. But first, let's look back. What you are about to read may be painful...but it is true.

Listen to Raul Hillberg, a foremost scholar of the Holocaust:

> Since the fourth century after Christ there have been three anti-Jewish policies: [forced] conversion, expulsion, annihilation. The second appeared as an alternative to the first, and the third emerged as an alternative to the second....The missionaries of Christianity had said in effect: You have no right to live among us as Jews. The secular rulers who followed proclaimed: You have no right to live among us. The Nazis at last decreed: You have no right to live.

> The process began with the attempt to drive the Jews into Christianity. The development was continued in order to force the victims into exile. It was finished when the Jews were driven to their deaths. The German Nazis, then, did not discard the past; they built upon it. They did not begin a development; they completed it.[3]

Of course, Israel has not been perfect and blameless. The Bible itself is filled with words of rebuke for God's chosen people. The Lord told Moses that Israel was "stiff-necked" (Exod. 32:9) and He informed the prophet Ezekiel that if He had sent him to the Gentile nations *they* would have listened to him. "But the house of Israel is not willing to listen to you because they are not willing to listen to Me, for the whole house of Israel is hardened and obstinate" (Ezek. 3:7). The gospels record conflict after conflict between Jesus and the leaders of His people, and the Book of Acts states that the first believers were persecuted by abusive Jewish groups.[4]

But—and this is something we must fully grasp— Moses, Ezekiel, all the prophets, all the apostles and Jesus Himself *were all Israelites*. In fact, every "charter member" of the New Testament Church was born a Jew and died a Jew! (Jesus took this one step further: Jesus was born a Jew, died a Jew and was *resurrected* a Jew.) All the rebukes, all the criticisms, all the reproofs levelled against the Jewish people in the Scriptures were brought by their own kinsmen. All of it stayed within the family. And the reason God took a special interest in disciplining Israel was simple: He was treating him as a son! "This is what the Lord says: Israel is My firstborn son" (Exod. 4:22); and "what son is not disciplined by his father? If you are not disciplined (and everyone undergoes discipline), then you are illegitimate children and not true sons" (Heb. 12:7-8).

The Jews were—and are—chosen and loved by the Lord. God's chastisement of His people is a special sign of His love for them. They were called into a unique relationship with Him; therefore, they were, and are, accountable. Sonship is a great privilege. It carries great responsibility. To paraphrase the popular Jewish saying, "So who asked to be chosen?"

But the early Church quickly lost sight of Israel's special role and of the Father's covenantal love for His firstborn son. Soon an anti-Jewish cancer had infected her ranks. *The disease is still spreading today.* Consider just how much venom has poisoned Messiah's Body. After reading these quotes you will have a better idea why the Church has been—and still is—so sick.

Let's go all the way back to the fourth century. Our subject is none other than Saint John Chrysostom, a man described by Cardinal Newman as, "A bright cheerful gentle soul, a sensitive heart, a temperament open to emotion and impulse; and all this elevated, refined, transformed by the touch of heaven,—such a man was St. John Chrysostom."[5] He was known as one of the most eloquent preachers of truth and love; his very name, Chrysostom, means "golden-mouthed." This man was esteemed as one of the greatest of the "Church Fathers." But somehow all his compassion, all his sensitivity and gentleness were lost in dealing with the Jewish people. According to Chrysostom:

> The synagogue is worse than a brothel...it is the den of scoundrels and the repair of wild beasts...the temple of demons devoted to idolatrous cults...the refuge of brigands and debauchees, and the cavern of devils. [It is] a criminal assembly of Jews...a place of meeting for the assassins of Christ...a house worse than a drinking shop...a den of thieves; a house of ill fame, a dwelling of iniquity, the refuge of devils, a gulf and abyss of perdition.

As for the Jewish people themselves Chrysostom commented, "I would say the same things about their souls."

And so, "As for me, I hate the synagogue....I hate the Jews for the same reason."[6]

What happened to Christian love? Paul had wished that he could be cursed in place of his Jewish people. Chrysostom instead cursed them! How much destruction was subsequently ignited by these tragic sermons of malice? The Catholic historian Malcolm Hay is surely right when he says, "For many centuries the Jews listened to the echo of those three words of St. John Chrysostom, the Golden-Mouthed: 'God hates you.' "[7] And thus, "the popular Christian doctrine has always been that anyone, whether pagan or Christian, who has at any time persecuted, tortured or massacred Jews has acted as an instrument of Divine wrath."[8]

During the long, dark years of the Middle Ages, Jews were frequently given the option of baptism or expulsion, baptism or torture, baptism or death. Every type of degrading law was passed against them: They were forbidden to work good jobs; after all, they were an accursed people, assassins of Christ, so how could they be allowed to prosper? They were forced to listen to humiliating public sermons aimed at their conversion—wasn't this the holy obligation of the Church? Their children were kidnapped and baptized as "Christians," thus saving them from the fires of hell. They were rounded up and beaten as a highlight of Easter celebrations, since they deserved it as murderers of the Lord. And in the fervor and fanaticism of the Crusades, as the riffraff of Europe gathered to "liberate" the Holy Land from the Muslim infidels, a great new discovery was made: There were infidels that could be killed in their own backyard! Why wait for the Holy Land? And so the hideous slogan was born: "Kill a Jew and save your soul!"[9] (This sounds awfully similar to the Russian words that became popular last century: *"Byay Zhidov Spassai Rossiyu,"* "Beat the Jews [Zhids] and save Russia!"[10])

And what were the Church leaders saying about all this? It is true that the Jews had some friends among the Catholic clergy, and the names Bernard of Clairvaux and Pope Innocent III stand out. These men sought to stop the mass murders of innocent Jewish men, women and children. But how did they really feel about the Jews?

Bernard—one of the most influential monks who ever lived, almost legendary for his great love for God and for man—charged the whole Jewish people with "a stupidity bestial and more than bestial," an "intelligence coarse, dense, and as it were bovine," because they did not follow the Lord. They were an "evil seed"; there was nothing in them that was "not crude and coarse, whether we consider their occupations, their inclinations, their understanding, or even their rites [with] which they worship God." They were "a race who had not God for their father, but were of the devil, and were murderers as he was a murderer from the beginning."[11] This was from a "friend" of the Jews!

Peter the Venerable, a contemporary of Bernard known as "the meekest of men, a model of Christian charity," considered "the most peace-loving man of his time. A man of boundless charity,"[12] breathed an ugly spirit of Jew hatred:

> You, you Jews. I say, do I address you; you, who till this very day, deny the Son of God. How long, poor wretches, will ye not believe the truth? Truly I doubt whether a Jew can be really human....I lead out from its den a monstrous

animal, and show it as a laughing stock in the amphitheatre of the world, in the sight of all the people. I bring thee forward, thou Jew, thou brute beast, in the sight of all men.[13]

It is only a small step from this description of the Jew as a "monstrous animal" to the medieval representation of the Jew as a little devil, complete with horns and tails. Not surprisingly, these images were utilized by the Nazis.[14]

And let us not forget the unique contribution made by Innocent III, the Pope who was the protector of the Jewish people. According to him, the Jews were condemned to perpetual slavery "because they crucified the Lord."

The Jews, against whom the blood of Jesus Christ calls out, although they ought not to be killed, lest the Christian people forget the Divine Law, yet as wanderers ought they to remain upon the earth, until their countenance be filled with shame.[15]

For the Pope, the continued misery of these crucifiers of the Lord was a testimony to the truth of the Christian faith; therefore, by all means they must be degraded.

According to Malcolm Hay:

Trade boycott, social ostracism, expulsion from all offices of authority and trust, were the chief economic weapons [Pope Innocent] was able to use effectively against them.[16]

But all this was nothing new. What *was* new was the addition of the badge of shame: a distinctive badge "that they must wear on their clothing...like lepers or prostitutes." Thus the Jews were consigned

to wander over the face of the earth, without rights, except by gracious concession, without a home, and without security; treated at all times, in years of peace and in years of persecution, as if they were beings of an inferior species.[17]

In light of all this, it comes as no surprise that Martin Luther, in his breaking away from the Catholic Church, reached out kindly to the Jews. He emphasized that Jesus was born a Jew and hoped,

> Perhaps I will attract some of the Jews to the Christian faith. For our fools—the popes, bishops, sophists, and monks— the coarse blockheads! have until this time so treated the Jews that...if I had been a Jew and had seen such idiots and blockheads ruling and teaching the Christian religion, I would rather have been a sow than a Christian. For they have dealt with the Jews as if they were dogs and not human beings.[18]

This was written in 1523. Twenty years later, when the Jews did not convert *en masse,* when Luther was old and sick, and after seeing some blasphemous anti-Christian literature written by Jewish pens, he had a change of heart: "What shall we Christians do with this damned, rejected race of Jews?"

Luther's answer was decisive:

> First, their synagogues should be set on fire...Secondly, their homes should likewise be broken down and destroyed....Thirdly, they should be deprived of their prayer-books and Talmuds...Fourthly, their rabbis must be forbidden under threat of death to teach any more...Fifthly, passport and traveling privileges should be absolutely forbidden to the Jews....Sixthly, they ought to be stopped from usury [charging interest on loans]....Seventhly, let the young and strong Jews and Jewesses be given the flail, the

ax, the hoe, the spade, the distaff, and spindle, and let them earn their bread by the sweat of their noses...We ought to drive the rascally lazy bones out of our system....Therefore away with them....

To sum up, dear princes and nobles who have Jews in your domains, if this advice of mine does not suit you, then find a better one so that you and we may all be free of this insufferable devilish burden—the Jews.[19]

Later Lutherans repudiated these despicable remarks, just as the Catholic Church recently repudiated much of her anti-Jewish bias.[20] But something that was so widespread, so deep, so infecting and polluting, such venomous hatred and prejudice, does not die quickly. In 1933 the German Lutheran Gerhard Kittel, one of the great New Testament scholars of the day—his New Testament theological dictionary is on the shelves of virtually every seminary library in the world—published a book outlining how his country must handle the "Jewish question." Extermination would be impractical. (Later he added that it would also be unchristian.) Zionism was out of the question. (There were too many Jews to fit in Palestine, and the Arabs would not be happy with the situation anyway.) Assimilation would be the worst solution of all. That would corrupt the German race!

Rather, the Jews should accept discrimination and defamation as their lot. Let them be treated as "guests" in a foreign land—second class, beleaguered guests, of course. After all, they were Jews, weren't they? In fact, according to Kittel, the only authentic Jews were those...

who in obedience...take on themselves the suffering of dispersal....authentic Judaism abides by the symbol of the stranger wandering restless and homeless on the face of the earth.[21]

This was the carefully considered answer of a great Christian theologian!

In the words of Robert P. Ericksen, Kittel

resurrected Christian antisemitism from the Middle Ages, refurbished it with a touch of contemporary racial mysticism, and raised it as a German, Christian bulwark against the Jewish menace....[He] proposed harsh measures to deal with [this menace], and he directed his research to reveal Jewish degeneracy. In short, he swam in the Nazi stream, though he may have preferred a different stroke.[22]

That stream ended in the murder of two-thirds of Europe's Jews. The Nazis had indeed found a better way to be "free of this insufferable devilish burden—the Jews."[23]

Sadly and to our shame, we could go on and on with sickening quotation after quotation, with example after example of bitter Jew-hatred among the leaders of the "Church."[24] But we have already heard enough. Now it is time to stop and reflect: Could it be that the words of one so powerfully used as Martin Luther—a man whose writings sparked the Protestant Reformation, whose great genius deeply impacted the German intellect, whose commentaries on Romans and Galatians helped bring about the conversions of John and Charles Wesley, whose sensitive pen produced the precious hymn "A Mighty Fortress Is Our God"—could it be that *his* words helped stoke the fires of the Nazi extermination ovens?

Let the saints and popes and Luther himself arise from their graves and weep.

The Church has blood on her hands.

Chapter Three

A Blessed and
Beautiful Stream

It is true that the Church has sinned terribly against the Jewish people. *But not all the Church has sinned.* Wherever Jesus has been lifted up and adored, there have always been genuine lovers of Israel. There *has* been a bloody river of Jew-hatred that has flowed through the history of the Church. But there has also been a stream of sacrificial love. It must overflow its banks in our day. Mercy and compassion must arise for the Lord's brothers and sisters in the flesh. How exhilarating it is when we walk in love!

Consider the testimony of the Puritans. They sought to go back to the Word of God and to separate themselves from the dead traditions of men. They preached the need for individual salvation and holy living. They helped shape the American colonies. And many of them had a special love for Israel.[1]

John Owen, the greatest of the Puritan theologians, lived from 1616 to 1683. At that time there was no glimmer of hope, no possibility, of the Jews returning to their land. But John Owen believed the Scriptures. He wrote:

> The Jews shall be gathered from all parts of the earth where they are scattered, and brought home into their homeland.

As to their importance in God's plan, Owen wrote these amazing words:

> There is not any promise anywhere of raising up a kingdom unto the Lord Jesus Christ in this world but it is either expressed, or clearly intimated, that the beginning of it must be with the Jews.[2]

Robert Leighton, a contemporary of Owen, wrote:

> They forget a main point for the Church's glory, who pray not daily for the conversion [turning] of the Jews....Undoubtedly, that people of the Jews shall once more be commanded to *arise* and *shine,* and their return shall be the riches of the Gentiles (Romans 11:12), and that shall be a more glorious time than ever the Church of God did yet behold.[3]

Samuel Rutherford, the Puritan remembered most for his deep passion for the Lord, bared his heart in the hundreds of letters he wrote. Of these letters Charles Spurgeon said,

> When we are dead and gone let the world know that Spurgeon held Rutherford's Letters to be the nearest thing to inspiration which can be found in all the writings of mere men.[4]

Another godly author testified of Rutherford's Letters, saying that, with the exception of the Bible, "such a book the world never saw."[5]

What made Rutherford's writings so special? He was deeply in love with Jesus, and he knew the heartbeat of his

Savior. In every way, he wanted to bring joy to his Master. Because Jesus loved His own, Rutherford loved them too. *He knew that the Jews had a special place in the Kingdom of God.* Was Samuel Rutherford bigoted and misled?

More than anything else, Rutherford longed to be with Jesus. He yearned to see the Master face to face. But he was willing to wait and put off that day if he could be allowed to witness one thing:

> I could stay out of heaven many years to see that victorious triumphing Lord act that prophesied part of His soul-conquering love, in taking into His kingdom the greater sister, that kirk [church] of the Jews...Oh, what joy and what glory would I judge it, if my heaven should be suspended till I might have leave to run on foot to be a witness of that marriage-glory, and see Christ put on the glory of His last-married bride, and His last marriage love on earth; when He shall enlarge His love-bed, and set it upon the top of the mountains, and take in the Elder Sister, the Jews, and the fulness of the Gentiles![6]

Aside from Jesus' return to earth, Rutherford could think of nothing more glorious than Israel's restoration:

> O to see the sight, next to Christ's Coming in the clouds, the most joyful! Our elder brethren the Jews and Christ fall upon one another's neck and kiss each other! They have been long asunder; they will be kind to one another when they meet. O day! O longed-for and lovely day-dawn! O sweet Jesus, let me see that sight which will be as life from the dead, Thee and Thy ancient people in mutual embraces.[7]

Love like this can be produced only by the Holy Spirit. It comes from having God's heart. *If believers today walked in greater harmony with the Spirit and in greater*

*understanding of the Lord's heart, they would likely catch
God's burden for Israel too.*

There was a beautiful stream that flowed among the
Scottish Presbyterians last century. Foremost among them
was Robert Murray M'Cheyne, a young pastor whose
reputation for godliness was second to none. He was a man
of sensitivity and compassion. He prayed with tears and
preached with tears. His very presence often convicted
people of sin and revealed the forgiveness of the Lord.
His life story, with his sermons and letters, has touched
millions of believers worldwide. And with all his being,
M'Cheyne loved the Jews.

In 1839, after returning from a Jewish mission to Palestine, he preached a sermon from Romans 1:16 called: "Our
Duty to Israel." His message was, simply, *"That the gospel
should be preached first to the Jews."* Why?

> (1)Because judgment will begin with them...(2)It is like
> God to care first for the Jews....(3)Because there is peculiar
> access [to preach the gospel] to the Jews [throughout the
> world]....(4)Because they will give life to the dead world.[8]

The reconciliation of the Jews would mean the resurrection
of the dead!

These Presbyterians were convinced that, as far as Israel
was concerned, "Blessed is he that blesseth thee." So in
1839, when revival broke out in the Scottish city of Kilsyth
through the preaching of William C. Burns, M'Cheyne and
his contemporaries felt they knew why. There had been
much prayer, fasting and sacrifice. There had been a powerful proclamation of the cross. But there was something

else: 1839 was the year of the Jewish mission to Palestine! That's why special blessing came. That's why the Spirit was poured out.[9] *M'Cheyne was sure that this was to be a lasting pattern*: The salvation of the Jewish people meant restoration for the Church.

According to Andrew Bonar, speaking in 1889:

> Israel is the "everlasting nation" who are to be life from the dead to all nations. And the sure word of prophecy declares, "He that scattereth Israel shall gather them." "I will give them one heart and one way, that they may fear Me for ever." "Yea, I will rejoice over them, and will plant them in their own land assuredly, with all My heart, and with all My soul."

> Crowned with her fairest hope, the Church
> Shall triumph with her Lord,
> And earth her jubilee shall keep,
> When Israel is restored.[10]

What a day that will be!

M'Cheyne believed that if we would be evangelistic "*as God would have us to be*—[to] not only dispense the light on every hand, but dispense it first to the Jew," then we would see the same outpouring in our day and in our land that he witnessed in Kilsyth in 1839.

> Then shall God revive His work in the midst of the years. Our whole land shall be refreshed as Kilsyth has been. The cobwebs of controversy shall be swept out of our sanctuaries, the jarrings and jealousies of our Church be turned into the harmony of praise, and our own souls become like a well-watered garden.[11]

All this through preaching first to the Jew!

These godly Scotsmen tapped into that blessed stream. Look at the refreshing it gave!

But this stream of love toward the lost sheep of the house of Israel did not just flow in seventeenth century England and nineteenth century Scotland. In every generation there has been a godly remnant of Gentiles (a Gentile simply means someone from the nations, not from Israel) praying for the peace of Jerusalem. They have understood the words of Paul: As a result of God's mercy to them, the Jewish people can receive mercy too (Rom. 11:31).

There have been people like the ten-Boom family, who risked their lives, even sacrificed their lives, to rescue Jews from the hands of the Nazis.[12] And there have been others like Basilea Schlink, the German Lutheran nun, who together with the sisters in her order, have spent years in intercessory repentance for the grievous sins of their people.[13]

There have been famous missionaries like William Carey and Henry Martyn, who, when "tempted to weariness, thought thankfully of the promise of the Jews' ingathering."[14] There have been leaders like Charles Simeon, recognized as the preeminent Cambridge preacher from 1782 to 1836, a man deeply in love with the Jews. Iain Murray relates:

> Once at a missionary meeting Simeon had seemed so carried away with the future of the Jews that a friend passed him a slip of paper with the question, "Six millions of Jews and six hundred millions of Gentiles—which is the most important?" Simeon at once scribbled back, "If the conversion [turning] of the six is to be life from the dead to the six hundred, what then?"[15]

Bishop Handley C. G. Moule expressed this hope so well:

> The great event of Israel's return to God in Christ, and His to Israel, will be the signal and the means of a vast rise of spiritual life in the universal church, and of an unexampled ingathering of regenerate souls from the world.[16]

Only God knows how many unknown saints have wept and groaned in secret, longing for the day when "a fountain will be opened to the house of David and the inhabitants of Jerusalem, to cleanse them from sin and impurity" (Zech. 13:1).

They have cried out to the Lord for the opening of that fountain because it has already burst in their hearts.

*   *   *

There is a bitter, ugly stream that has flowed for many centuries through the Church. It flows to this very day. There is also a pure and holy stream of love.

Which stream flows in you?

Chapter Four

The Rabbis: Stiff-necked, Hardhearted and Proud?

There are hypocritical leaders in every religion. There are charlatans in every faith. But are the rabbis especially guilty? Are they worse than everyone else? Do they all conceal horrible sins in their hearts? Are they ungodly blasphemers, since they deny Jesus as Lord? Are they superficial legalists, since they reject the New Covenant? Let's look at some examples.

Rabbi Akiva, one of the most famous sages of the Talmud, died a martyr's death in the year 135.[1] He had made the tragic error of believing that a powerful Jewish general who rose up against Rome was actually the Messiah. But the Roman armies prevailed. The government quickly clamped down on the Jews, severely restricting their religious liberty. When the Romans banned the public teaching of the Law, Akiva refused to comply. He continued to teach in public, not even stopping while in prison. Finally the day for his torture and death arrived.

As the sadistic crowds looked on with glee, the executioner began to comb Akiva's 90-year-old flesh with iron combs. But Akiva's mind was on something else. The time had come to recite the *Shema,* the confession of faith outlawed by Rome, beginning with the words, "Hear O Israel, the Lord our God, the Lord is one." So he recited it and smiled.

> The Roman officer called out, "Old man, art thou a sorcerer, or dost thou mock at thy sufferings, that thou smilest in the midst of thy pains?" "Neither," replied Akiva, "but all my life, when I said the words, 'Thou shalt love the Lord thy God with all thy heart and soul and might,' I was saddened, for I thought, when shall I be able to fulfill the command? I have loved God with all my heart and with all my possessions [might], but how to love Him with all my soul [i.e. life] was not assured me. Now that I am giving my life, and that the hour for saying the *Shema* has come, and my resolution remains firm, should I not laugh?" And as he spoke, his soul departed.[2]

This became the pattern for countless Jewish martyrs who would follow in Akiva's steps. They died with the *Shema,* the Jewish confession of faith, on their lips.

Elchanan Wasserman was one of the greatest rabbis of Eastern Europe. In 1941 he met his death at the hands of the Nazi butchers. Rabbi Wasserman and a number of leading Jewish scholars were studying the Talmud together in the ghetto in Kovno, Lithuania, on July 6, 1941. Suddenly a group of Lithuanian fascists broke into the room, firing their rifles and accusing the rabbis of trying to organize a revolt. These crazed soldiers lined up the rabbis and began to march them to their death when Rabbi Wasserman stopped and addressed those with him:

> It appears that in Heaven they view us as *tzaddikim* [righteous men] worthy to atone with our lives for the people of Israel. We must, therefore, immediately repent here and now, for the time is short and the Ninth Fort [the place of execution] is near. We must remember that we will in truth be those who sanctify God's name. Let us therefore go with heads erect, let us, God forbid, have no unworthy thought, which like unfit intention, in the case of a sacrifice rendered it invalid. We are now about to fulfill the greatest commandment—that of sanctifying the Name. The fire which will destroy us is the flame out of which the Jewish people will be rebuilt.[3]

Moments later, Rabbi Wasserman and his colleagues were gone, machine gunned to death—but his dying words lived on. *The state of Israel was miraculously born out of the ashes of the Holocaust.*

Rabbi Wasserman's teacher was a man named Yisrael Meir HaCohen. His first great book was called: *Hafetz Hayyim* (also spelled *Chofetz Chayyim*), "He Who Desires Life." The title is taken from Psalm 34:12: "He who desires life and wants to see many good days, let him keep his tongue from evil and his lips from speaking lies." This book dealt with the Jewish laws against slander and gossip, and it became so famous that Rabbi Yisrael Meir HaCohen grew to be known as *the Chofetz Chayyim*. He practiced what he preached. In fact, it was said that he would not even lift his pen to sign his name on a delivery receipt without first saying, "For the glory of God." His conduct would put most of us to shame.[4]

On one occasion, it is told, a gentile peasant inadvertently left behind a small smoked fish, which he had purchased in the Chofetz Chaim's store. The Chofetz Chaim was deeply disturbed when he realized he would be unable to locate and identify the peasant who had purchased the fish. On the very next market day, therefore, the Chofetz Chaim distributed a free fish to every peasant who entered the store.[5]

What an example of business ethics!

The Chofetz Chaim taught that

this world is not a place of happiness for true joy is only in the heavens and we are here to do the job assigned to us by the Creator.[6]

He lived a life of sacrifice.

Our Sages say that G-d's throne is not complete as long as the Redemption has not yet come. So how can I sit on a comfortable easy chair when I know that G-d sits, as it were, on a broken chair?[7]

He believed in the mercy of the Lord.

If not for our good fortune that G-d has shown us the kindness of accepting our repentance we would drown in the mud we have created in only a few years.[8]

Does this sound like the writing of an arrogant man?

Some Christians think that the Talmud, the foundation of the rabbis' teaching, is a wicked and misleading book (actually, it consists of *many* books). They imagine that it is filled with horrible attacks on the New Testament and that every page smacks of Jewish arrogance and pride. But is this picture really true?

Out of the Talmud's two-and-a-half-million (2,500,000) words, hardly any of them mention Jesus or His followers. When Jesus apparently is referred to, the few references are decidedly negative.[9] This should not surprise us, since the rabbis did not believe in Him. But to be perfectly honest, most of the rabbis missed Him altogether. They built their own system *without* Him. They *ignored* Him more than they rejected Him. Basically, the Talmud is not an anti-Christian series of books! It is more *non*-Christian than *anti*-Christian, more *without* Jesus than *against* Jesus.[10] This should make us feel sad, not angry!

Of course, it is true that the Talmud has some harsh things to say about the Gentiles. But it also says some positive things about them (not to mention a lot of negative things that it says about its own people). The fact is still the same: The Talmud doesn't really make a big issue about the rest of the world. It is concerned mainly with how *Jews* should live here. As for everyone else, the rabbis taught that the righteous of every nation would have a place in the world to come. And while the Talmud is, in fact, filled with hundreds of pages of legal discussion that could make even a lawyer dizzy, it is also filled with beauty and wisdom.[11]

Here are some of the things it says.

How can we avoid coming under the power of transgression?

Contemplate these three things: Know what is above you— an all-seeing eye, an all-hearing ear, and all your deeds recorded in a book.[12]

How should we serve God?

Do not be like servants that minister to the master on the condition of receiving a reward, but be like servants that minister to the master without the condition of receiving a reward; and let the fear of heaven be upon you.[13]

How should we pray? (Remember, religious Jews pray from a prayer book, reading fixed, written prayers.)

He who makes his prayer a mechanical task, his prayer is not prayer....One should not pray in levity and jest, but in gravity and the joy of doing good....Prayer is greater than sacrifices....Prayer is the service of the heart....Prayer is acceptable only if the soul is offered with it.[14]

What is true repentance, and how powerful is it?

Whoever says, "I shall sin and repent, I shall sin and repent," repentance will not be vouchsafed him....Once a man repents, stop reminding him of what he did!...Great is repentance, for it brings healing to the world....Great is repentance, for it reaches the Throne of Glory;...for it brings Redemption;...for it lengthens a man's life....The Lord said: "I cannot bring Myself to look upon a wicked man, but if he repent, I shall crown him with a crown like unto Mine own."[15]

How much should a man love God?

What is the fitting love of God? It is that a man should love God with an extraordinary powerful love to the extent that his soul becomes tied to the love of God so that he pines for it unceasingly. It should be as if he were lovesick, unable to get the woman he loves out of his mind, pining for her all the time when he eats or drinks. Even more than this should be the love of God in the hearts of those who love Him and yearn constantly for Him, as He has commanded us, "with all your heart and with all your soul" (Deut. 6:5).[16]

What did the rabbis say about love for man?

All that you do, do only out of love![17]

We must change our stereotyped views about the Jewish religion. It *is* a religion of Law. It *is* a religion emphasizing works. It *is* a religion exalting intellectual prowess and study. It *is* a religion stressing legal argument and debate. But it is the greatest religion man has made, the greatest effort by human beings to please God—*if it were in man's power to please Him.* With all my heart, I believe that there were and are religious Jews who would be counted righteous before God, *if it were possible for man on his own to be righteous.*

Of course, it is not. Only through the Messiah's blood can we be redeemed. Only through His merits can we be saved. Without Him, we are, at best, a fallen race trying very hard. But trying very hard is not enough. Even asking for God's mercy, as every religious Jew does every day, is not enough. We need a totally transforming miracle of God's grace. *Jesus is that miracle.* The rabbis need Him too.

Then how should we view these men? How should we think about the religious Jew? Some might be hypocrites, filled with spiritual pride. Some rabbis might be rabbis just because they think it's a good job. But others might be totally sincere. Like Paul, they might be "faultless" as far as "legalistic righteousness" is concerned (Phil. 3:6). They may even live a better life than many of us! "For I can testify about them that they are zealous for God, but their zeal is not based on knowledge" (Rom. 10:2). They are zealous to this very day.

Let us not be so quick to judge and condemn. Instead, let us share our faith in compassion. Let us open our hearts to God, asking Him to break our hearts in prayer; for in spite of all their study, in spite of all their devotion, in spite of all their efforts, the lost sheep of the house of Israel are still lost.

Pray that their Shepherd would find them.

Chapter Five

Miriam and Jacob: Household Names in the Savior's Home

What do you think of when you hear the words, "Mary, the mother of Jesus"? Do you think of a statue in a Catholic church somewhere, with the Son of God as a babe in His mother's lap? It certainly sounds "Christian," doesn't it? Now, what do you think of when you hear the words, "Miriam, the mother of Yeshua"? Quite a different picture comes to mind! This one looks extremely Jewish.

Well, for the record: *The mother of Jesus was named Miriam as surely as the sister of Moses was named Miriam.* In fact, all the Mary's in the New Testament were Jewish women called Miriam. (That's right, Mary Magdalene was actually Miriam of Magdala! If we had called her "Mary," she would not have known we were talking to her.) Because the New Testament was written in Greek, the names have come down to us in Greek dress. But, if we want to get our facts straight, we need to understand that John was really Jochanan (pronounced Yochanan), Matthew was really Mattityahu (Mattai for short) and good ol' Simon Peter was really Shimon Kepha.[1] In fact, James, the Lord's brother and author of the Epistle of James, was really not James at all. He was Jacob! Even in the Greek his name was written as Jacob; but somehow, in our English Bibles, it became James.[2]

Now, let's pick up our New Testaments and begin reading again. All of a sudden it's a different book. Our Savior and Lord is named *Yeshua*. (When this name occurs in our English Old Testaments, it is spelled Jeshua.[3]) His mother is Miriam; His earthly father is Joseph. (It was pronounced Yoseph, but Yeshua would have called him "Abba.") He also has a brother named Judah, the author of the Epistle of Judah (Jude).

His disciples sound like an altogether new group. Among them are Jacob and Jochanan, the sons of Zavdai (Zebedee) and someone called Bar Talmai (ever heard of Bartholomew?). The languages they speak are primarily Aramaic and Hebrew (very similar to what Ezra and Nehemiah spoke 500 years earlier, or Jacob more than a thousand years before that). Most everywhere they go has a Jewish sound to it: the village of Nahum (Kefar Nahum— Capernaum), Beth Ani (Bethany) and Natzeret (Nazareth).[4]

Yeshua's disciples call Him "Rabbi," He attends synagogue on the Sabbath and He even dresses as a biblical Jew: When the woman with the issue of blood reached out for her healing, she touched the *fringe* of His garment

(Matt. 15:20; Num. 15:38-39. It's the same word in Greek!).[5] Until the very end of His life, no one could accuse Him of breaking the written Law. The Son of God lived His days on earth as a totally observant Jew.[6] He differed with the traditions of men, not with the Torah (teaching, law) of God. He was hailed as "King of the Jews" when He came into the world; He was mocked as "King of the Jews" when He hung upon the cross. *He never disputed the title.*[7]

Now, let's flip toward the back of the Bible and stop right before the letters of Peter. Are you ready to read the Epistle of Jacob? (That's right, say it out loud: "I'm going to read the Epistle of Jacob.") But no sooner have you begun to read when you come upon another surprise. Look at who it is written to: "To the twelve tribes scattered among the nations." He's writing to Jewish believers living outside their Land! *This is Jacob's letter to the Jews.* (If someone ever told us that "the twelve tribes" meant "the whole Church"—Gentile and Jew— they were wrong.) All of Jacob's references to the Law now take on a whole new light![8]

Of course, every child of God can apply this letter to himself, just as we can all apply Paul's letter to the Corinthians to our own situations today. But as surely as Paul wrote letters to the Colossians, Romans, Philippians, Thessalonians, Galatians and Corinthians, Jacob wrote this letter to the Jews. *If you find yourself upset about that, ask God to help you search your heart. Maybe there's some anti-Jewishness there.*

Paul's case provides us with a classic example of unconscious, anti-Jewish attitudes. This is the way many think: Before Paul knew the Lord, he was *Saul* (in other words, he was Jewish). Once he was born again, he became *Paul* (in other words, he was now Christian). So Saul (= Jewish) is bad and Paul (= Christian) is good. Isn't this simple and clear?

Not at all! It's not even correct. He was Saul before his Damascus road experience in Acts 9 and he was Saul *after* his Damascus road experience. That's right, meet the *apostle Saul* (in Hebrew, Sha'ul). Even after he was sent out by the brothers in Acts 13 (this is when some people believe he first "became" an apostle) he was still called Saul. It is only later in Acts 13 that we are told he was *also* called Paul (in other words, like most Roman Jews in his day, he had more than one name).[9] There is no reason to think that he was called Paul by his Jewish brothers, who spoke to him in Hebrew or Aramaic. Why would they use his Greek (or Roman) name? That was what he used when writing and teaching in Greek. To the believers in Israel, he was always their beloved brother Saul. Now let's try that one on for size: The greatest apostle who ever lived was a Jew named Saul.

Yeshua the Messiah, Miriam His mother, the Epistle of Jacob and the apostle Saul. The gospel grew out of very Jewish soil! But there's much more to say.

The famous phrase "Maranatha" is not Greek; it's Aramaic. It was the heart cry of the Jewish believers (most probably *marana tha*, "Our Lord, come!") and it became the universal language of the early church. When Jesus taught us to address God as "Abba," He was simply saying, "Do what I have done. *Do what every Jewish boy does.* Call your Father Abba! You have been adopted into His family."

Our most intimate prayer term, "Abba!" and our most fervent prayer request, "Maranatha!" are both good Jewish expressions. Being a Christian is more Jewish than we knew!

Of course, most of us realize that the roots of our faith are Jewish. But did we ever stop to consider that *Jewish roots mean Jewish fruit?* Our faith not only began in Israel, with the Jewish people in the middle of everything, but it will also end in Israel with the Jewish people in the middle of everything.

Let's look at the main holy days that God gave to His people. They are filled with prophetic meaning and spiritual truth. In the first month, on the fourteenth day of the month, the *Passover* celebration began. Then, on the first Sunday after Passover, there was the celebration of *Firstfruits.* Fifty days after Passover came the *Feast of Weeks (Pentecost).*

Outside of Sabbaths and New Moons, there were no other holy days until the seventh month. *The first three holy days speak of the Lord's first coming; the last three holy days speak of His return.*[10] That's why such a long gap is between them.

On the first day of the seventh month the *Feast of Trumpets* was held (this later became the Jewish New Year). Ten days later was the *Day of Atonement;* then five days after that came the *Feast of Tabernacles.*

The death of Jesus coincided with *Passover.* (Remember, He was the Lamb of God!) His resurrection coincided with *Firstfruits.* "But Christ has indeed been raised from the dead, the *firstfruits* of them who have fallen asleep" (1 Cor. 15:20). The Holy Spirit was poured out on the *Feast of Weeks* (Pentecost).

The gospel began with the first three holy days of Israel. *It will end with the last three holy days of Israel.*

The return of Jesus will coincide prophetically with the *Feast of Trumpets.*

> They will see the Son of Man coming on the clouds of the sky, with power and great glory. And He will send His angels with a *loud trumpet call...* (Matt. 24:30-31)

> We will not all sleep, but we will all be changed—in a flash, in the twinkling of an eye, *at the last trumpet.* For the trumpet will sound, the dead will be raised imperishable, and we will be changed (1 Cor. 15:51-52).

> For the Lord Himself will come down from heaven, with a loud command, with the voice of the archangel *and with the trumpet call of God,* and the dead in Christ will rise first (1 Thess. 4:16).

Jesus will come back with the blast of the trumpet!

Zechariah tells us that when the Jewish people see their crucified Messiah, they will mourn deeply in repentance (Zech. 12:10).

> On that day a fountain will be opened to the house of David and the inhabitants of Jerusalem, to cleanse them from sin and impurity (Zech. 13:1).

It will be a national Day of Atonement. Forgiveness will finally come!

The Word is wonderfully clear. First came the Passover (Jesus' death), Firstfruits (His resurrection) and Pentecost (the outpouring of the Spirit). Then will be Trumpets (the second coming), Atonement (national forgiveness) and only one festival will remain: Tabernacles—celebrating the final ingathering of the harvest!

After the Lord returns and Israel receives atonement, "the survivors from all the nations that have attacked Jerusalem [in the final end-time war] will go up year after year to worship the King, the LORD Almighty, *and to celebrate the Feast of Tabernacles*" (Zech. 14:16).

All the nations will celebrate the Feast of Tabernacles in Jerusalem every year! At that time this Scripture will be fulfilled:

> In those days ten men from all languages and nations will take firm hold of one Jew by the hem of his robe and say, "Let us go with you, because we have heard that God is with you" (Zech. 8:23).

People from all over the world will come streaming up to the mountain of the Lord. They won't say, "Let's go up to Rome, or Tulsa, or Dallas, or Seoul." No! They'll say, "Let's go up to *Jerusalem!*" They won't say, "Let's go up to First Baptist, or Second Presbyterian, or Full Gospel Assembly." Instead they'll say, "Let's go up to the house of the *God of Jacob!*" For "the Law will go out from Zion, the word of the LORD from Jerusalem" (Is. 2:1-4).

And do you know what the final blow to anti-Semitism will be?

The One who plants His feet on the Mount of Olives will be a glorified Jew.[11]

Chapter Six

Bad Reporting, Bias and Bigotry

What do the major newspapers, news magazines and news broadcasts on television and radio all have in common? It is a history of misleading, anti-Israel reporting! Here are some glaring examples.

A photo was released by United Press International on August 2, 1982, during the heat of the Israeli-PLO conflict in Lebanon.

> The photo showed a 7-month-old Lebanese girl swathed in bandages from head to foot. The caption that accompanied the picture said the child had lost both arms and had been severely burned in the "accidental bombing" of an apartment house in East Beirut by the Israeli Air Force. Outraged, President Reagan put in a personal telephone call to Premier Begin urging him to suspend the Israeli bombing of PLO targets in West Beirut, using the word "holocaust" in the ensuing exchange.[1]

Naturally this touching photograph received front page coverage everywhere, making the Israelis look like cold-blooded killers. Just think of their brutal, indiscriminate attack on helpless civilians! Unfortunately, while the media was quick to focus on the Israeli Defense Forces' mistakes, (they made their share of mistakes in Lebanon), the media was slow to report the rest of the facts.

How many Americans were told that a significant portion of the Lebanese populace greeted the Israeli troops with flowers, thanking them for finally driving the PLO out of their land?[2] How many Americans realized that the Yasser Arafat who appeared on TV screens kissing babies and little children was the same terrorist who gave his hooligans orders to torture, mutilate and slaughter anyone who got in his way?[3]

"But what about that 7-month-old baby?" you say. "That was still a terrible crime." Here again the true story was suppressed. Frank Gervasi tells us that after Reagan's phone call, the Israeli authorities

> made a thorough investigation, and on August 22 released a photo of the same child after treatment. The infant had *not* lost both arms, and had suffered no burns and only slight injuries to the wrists. Moreover, the baby, it turned out, was not hurt by an Israeli bomb but by a shell from a PLO battery in West Beirut. The UPI confirmed that the original caption was inaccurate and expressed regret. But whereas the original photo was splashed everywhere, the corrected version barely made the inside pages (The *New York Times* printed it on page 14).[4]

It seems that some people are not even *trying* to report fairly!

Today there is much talk about the "Palestinian problem," and there are calls for the immediate creation of a

Palestinian state within Israel. Yet, while the plight of these refugees is tragic, and while they do need our prayers for a righteous solution to be found, an ugly double standard is being used. Where was the world outcry—from the United Nations, from the U.S. Senate, from the media—when Jordan killed more than 3,400 of its own Palestinians during just ten days of the infamous Black September riots of 1970, or when Syria slaughtered 23,000 Palestinians in 1976?[5] (By the way, with all the talk about forming a Palestinian state in the Middle East, people seem to have forgotten that there already is one. It's called Jordan! More than half of Jordan's people are Palestinians.[6])

When 19 Arabs were shot to death during the Temple Mount uprising October 8, 1990, the U.N., with the agreement of America, soundly condemned Israel's use of force. But where was the condemnation a few days later when Syrian troops raped and massacred several hundred Lebanese Christians after the Lebanese had surrendered?[7] (Of course, this is no surprise. The U.N. Security Counsel did not respond to Syria's killing as many as 30,000 of its civilians in Hama, Syria, in 1982; the Soviet occupation of Afghanistan; the Tienammen Square massacre in China; or the Iraqi Air Force's gassing of 8,000 Kurds in 1988-1989, to mention only a few. But let Israel make one wrong move, and the U.N. is in an uproar!)

As for the Temple Mount uprising, the whole story was hardly told. According to most of the news coverage, the Muslims spontaneously rioted when they heard that a small group of extremist Jews was coming that day to lay the foundation stone for the building of the third Temple.

Erecting the new Temple would be a threat to the great Islamic Dome of the Rock and Al-'Aqsa Mosque, built on the very same site.

But there was no need for anyone to panic. The Israeli government had banned the little Jewish group from going anywhere near the Temple Mount. They announced this fact several days in advance, notified the Arabic newspapers and printed special flyers. They even met with the key Muslim officials to make sure everything was clear!

No, this was not a spontaneous riot. The huge piles of rocks that were utilized by the stone-throwers did not just materialize out of thin air. This was a pre-planned attempt to make Israel look bad, even if it cost some lives.[8] It worked like a charm for the Palestinian cause. Once more the world was upset with Israel.

But the world is always getting upset with Israel.

In 1973, *just four days after the Arabs attacked Israel on Yom Kippur,* the Day of Atonement, the Security Council of the United Nations "exploded into prolonged applause" (this in itself was highly unusual) when Yakov Malik of the Soviet Union called the Israelis "murderers and international gangsters."[9] Then, on October 1, 1975, the infamous Idi Amin of Uganda, already well known as a savage mass murderer and cannibal who ate the refrigerated body parts of his victims, addressed the United Nations and received a standing ovation from the U.N. General Assembly, both before and after his speech. His message? He denounced "The Zionist-American conspiracy" and called for the expulsion of Israel from the

U.N., as well as Israel's *extinction.* "The next day the U.N. Secretary General gave a public dinner in his honor."[10]

In our very own congressional halls, on January 18, 1991, just two days after the Persian Gulf War erupted and only hours after Iraq's Scud Missiles had exploded in Tel Aviv, Illinois Congressman Gus Savage somehow found fuel for his anti-Israel fire. In a speech delivered before the House of Representatives—and aired live nationally—he equated Iraq's unprovoked bombing of civilians in Israel the previous night with Israel's bombing of Iraq's *nuclear weapon plant* in 1981! While he deplored Iraq's actions, he wondered where our national outcry had been when Israel destroyed Iraq's nuclear capabilities. What would the Middle East look like today if Israel had allowed Saddam Hussein to have nuclear bombs at his fingertips?

Of course, not every military action of Israel is justifiable. The Israelis at times have been guilty of excessive use of force and there have been instances of outright brutality. Certainly there are Israeli soldiers who have gotten out of control after months of confrontations with stone-throwing mobs, even beating several Palestinians to the point of death.[11] But where are the Israeli terrorists who have intentionally blown up buses filled with school children? (The PLO has done this.) Where is the list of Lebanese newspaper reporters who the Israelis have chopped up alive, joint by joint? (The PLO has done this.) Yet the PLO receives hundreds of millions of dollars in backing from nations like Saudi Arabia and Kuwait, and virtually no rebuke or censure from the U.N.[12]

It must be remembered also that, while terrorism is the *policy* of groups like the PLO (have you ever wondered what they do with their vast funding?[13]) terrorism is utterly denounced by Israel. The Israelis prosecute and punish their own people for unprovoked attacks against their enemies! Even before 1948, when a couple of Jewish terrorist groups fought in Palestine (they were totally outnumbered by Arab terrorist groups), their activities were soundly condemned by the Zionist leaders.[14] To this day, large segments of the Israeli media and government, together with Jewish leaders worldwide, openly criticize their countrymen for any army actions perceived as inhuman.[15] Yet in countries like Syria, torture is a routine procedure of interrogation and intimidation, carried out with the approval of the highest levels of military intelligence.[16]

During the conflict in Lebanon, Dr. Khalil Torbey, a distinguished Lebanese surgeon, reported cases "of people being thrown into acid tanks" by the PLO, not by Israel, "and reduced to unrecognizable masses of porous bone."

Dr. Torbey continues:

I treated persons with arms severed by shelling, and men whose testicles had been crushed by torturers [the work of the PLO, not of Israel]. I saw men—live men, mind you—dragged through the streets from fast-moving cars to which they were tied by their feet.

In fact, according to Frederick El-Murr, a leading Lebanese industrialist, a

favorite [PLO] method of ridding themselves of political opponents was to tie the feet of the male victims to separate cars speeding off in opposite directions.[17]

While these atrocities were taking place, Israeli generals were holding special meetings to discuss ways to minimize civilian casualties in Lebanon, even if this meant risking the lives of *Israeli* soldiers![18]

Many would have us believe that since Yasser Arafat's historic Geneva press conference on December 14, 1988, the PLO has recognized Israel's right to exist and renounced all acts of terrorism. But this is simply not true. Actually,

> the PLO renunciation of terror has had no tangible effect on PLO behavior. Infiltration attempts have continued, PLO death squads have continued to kill Palestinians [who resist their terrorist activities, slaughtering 315 as of December 9, 1990], and PLO leaders, including Arafat, continue to call for "armed struggle" against Israel.[19]

On May 18, 1989, Farouk Kaddoumi, head of the PLO's political department and the man in charge of the PLO's foreign affairs, was asked by a newspaper interviewer if Arafat "renounced terrorism in Geneva." He replied:

> That is a misrepresentation of Chairman Arafat's statements....We denounce terrorism, especially the state terrorism by Israel.

The interviewer then asked:

> Does that mean that the words that made [former Secretary of State George] Schultz begin a dialogue are null and void?

Kaddoumi replied:

> Schultz can go to hell. I suppose he is already on his way there.[20]

Do not be deceived; Israel is not the sinister force of the Middle East, the Jewish Goliath terrorizing its helpless little neighbors. Almost all Israelis long to live in peace, but their avowed Arab enemies, and much of the media as well, seem dead set against it.

This is not meant to absolve every Israeli troop. Some are not blameless by any means. And this is not meant to dismiss the needs of the Palestinians. They deserve our sympathy, especially since they are being used as pawns in a larger anti-Israel battle. We must also remember that the Arab nations are loved by God. Arab-hatred is no better than Jew-hatred. But it would be wonderful to see the media treat both sides fairly instead of constantly bashing the Jewish state! Let the *truth* be told in full. How tragic it is that the only way Israel can get any sympathy is by *losing* its wars! Why is Israel faulted for defending its own security instead of "turning the other cheek"?[21]

But there is something more disturbing than this media bias, because, despite so many reporters seemingly bent on making Israel look bad (even though some of the networks and papers are owned by liberal American Jewish groups), there is not much outright hostility or venom in their words. Yet there is plenty of venom in the frightening ideology that unites groups as diverse as White supremacists, Black militants and Muslim extremists.

What could these mutually contradictory factions possibly have in common? *They have great respect for Adolf Hitler and deep animosity toward the Jew.* They form an unholy alliance of hate. The observation of Methodist professor A. Roy Eckardt bears repeating:

Membership in the religion of anti-Semitism is ever open to all. It is the only universal faith. The language of anti-Semitism is the devil's native tongue; it quickly becomes the second language of the devil's disciples, and soon it takes command of their original language.... [The devil] is the god of anti-Semitism.[22]

Stokely Carmichael, the radical Black-power leader, said in 1970:

I have never admired a White man, but the greatest of them, to my mind, was Hitler.[23]

In a March 1984 radio broadcast, Louis Farrakhan, founder of the racist Nation of Islam, said:

the Jews don't like Farrakhan, so they call me Hitler. Well, that's a good name. Hitler was a very great name.

Speaking in Washington, D.C. in July 1985, Farrakhan stated that

Jews know their wickedness, not just Zionism, which is an outgrowth of Jewish transgression.[24]

Is it any wonder that Farrakhan and Libya's Muammar Khaddafi are good friends?[25]

The Jews, says Farrakhan, are "sucking the blood of the black community" (February 18, 1990, Michigan State University). But, he boasts, "The Jews cannot defeat me. I will grind them and crush them into little bits" (May 21, 1988, Flushing, New York).[26]

David Duke—former leader of the Ku Klux Klan, elected to Louisiana's state legislature, only narrowly defeated in his 1990 bid for a U.S. Senate seat and then elected as the (unsuccessful) Republican candidate for governor—called Hitler's *Mein Kampf* "the greatest piece of literature of the 20th century."[27] And Neo-Nazism is rapidly increasing today among virtually all phases of White supremacy movements, with swastikas, anti-Jewish violence and all.[28]

Willis Carto, founder of the Liberty Lobby that publishes *The Spotlight,* a weekly anti-Semitic tabloid with a circulation of almost 100,000, wrote:

> Hitler's defeat was the defeat of Europe. And of America. How could we have been so blind?...If Satan himself, with all of his superhuman genius and diabolical ingenuity at his command, had tried to create a permanent disintegration and force for the destruction of the nations, he could have done no better than to invent the Jews....The Jews...remain Public Enemy No. 1.[29]

This sounds very similar to the remark of Martin Luther:

> Know, Christian, that next to the devil thou hast no enemy more cruel, more venomous and violent than a true Jew.[30]

In recent issues, *The Spotlight* has praised Neo-Nazi skinheads for "their often violent displays of patriotism" and made note of their "macho creed with two-fisted values such as personal courage and fighting skills."[31]

The Anti-Defamation League points out:

> Liberty Lobby's outreach has also expanded overseas. Its program called "Radio Free America" is now carried on shortwave radio to Europe, South America, India and the Middle East by *World Wide Christian Radio,* a 100,000-watt station in Nashville, Tennessee.[32]

The September 1990 issue of *The Nationalist,* published by the "Voice of the National Democratic Front," blames

Hitler's European aggression on Franklin Delano Roosevelt, portrays Saddam Hussein as a well meaning, peace-seeking Arab hero and claims that our American boys will "die once again for the benefit of the Jews" in the Persian Gulf War.

> It is the Jews who now, once again, want Americans to do their fighting for them....Our gutless [politicians] know better than to oppose the Jews...and you can smell the stench of yellow journalism wafting from your television sets each evening and each morning as the Jewish controlled networks (ABC, NBC, CBS and PBS) pound the drums for war.[33]

As for the militant Muslim world, it certainly has not repudiated Hitler and his ways. Listen to some representative quotes:

> On August 17, 1956, the French newspaper *Le Monde* quoted the government-controlled Damascus daily *Al-Manar* as having written, "One should not forget that in contrast to Europe, Hitler occupied an honored place in the Arab world....his name makes us proud....Long live Hitler, the Nazi who struck at the heart of our enemies."

> On April 24, 1961, the Jordanian English-language daily *Jerusalem Times* published an "Open Letter to [Adolf] Eichmann" [shortly before his execution] which concluded, "But be brave, Eichmann, find solace in the fact that this trial will one day culminate in the liquidation of the remaining six million to avenge your blood."[34]

The founder of Saudi Arabia, Abdul Aziz was a friend of Hitler's Third Reich. He stated in 1937:

> Our hatred for the Jews dates from God's condemnation of them for their persecution and rejection of 'Isa [Jesus

Christ] and their subsequent rejection later of His chosen prophet [Muhammad]....[35]

Saudi leaders have followed in Abdul Aziz' footsteps; King Faisal highly praised the notoriously anti-Jewish book called *The Protocols of the Elders of Zion* (conclusively proved to be a forged work of lying propaganda) and gave it to all his international guests to read.[36] In 1972, he stated that "all countries should wage war against the Zionists."[37]

This echoes the cry sounded in 1948 by the Mufti of Jerusalem, Haj Amin Al-Husseini, a confidant of Hitler who spent much of World War II in Germany:

> The entire Jewish population in Palestine must be destroyed or be driven into the sea. Allah has bestowed on us the rare privilege of finishing what Hitler only began. Let the *Ji'had* begin. Murder the Jews. Murder them all![38]

This remains a sacred Arab mission to this day. As expressed by Jordan's King Hussein in 1967 during the Six Day War:

> Kill the Jews wherever you find them. Kill them with your arms, with your hands, with your nails and teeth.[39]

Yet, impossible as it may seem, there is something even more disturbing. Although bad reporting and bias in the media are hardly excusable, they are somewhat understandable. Who ever said newspeople were perfect saints? And although bigotry among racist groups and religious fanatics is appalling, when we stop to consider their beliefs and goals, it is only natural! What is *not* natural or excusable in any way is Church leaders and nationally read

Christian authors, people who profess to be born-again, Bible-believing Christians, now raising their voices in condemnation of the Jewish people in the Promised Land!

Oh yes, thank God for the large number of believers who love Israel, bless Israel and support her financially. It was Christian Zionists who travailed in prayer for Israel's national rebirth, and Christian Zionists today who remain active on all fronts, both spiritual and natural, to show their solidarity with the Jewish people and their land. But these are not the only voices being heard.

One pastor lays the blame for Arab-Israeli tensions squarely at Israel's door:

> Arab suspicion of Israeli expansionism coupled with the unresolved refugee problem keeps the Arab world in a constant offensive and defensive position.[40]

In other words, if only those Israelis would stop seeking to expand their kingdom, we would have peace!

Yet Israel is not trying to drive its Arab neighbors into the sea (or into the desert, as the case may be). It is simply trying to exist in peace and security. On the other hand, it is the stated intention of most of Israel's "neighbors" to drive the Jewish state into the sea! The problem is simply *not* one of "Israeli expansionism."[41]

Yet the charges against Israel grow still more ludicrous. The author of a book which was mailed free of charge to clergymen throughout the States claims that U.S. support for Israel has

> contributed to the frustration of Christian missionary activity in the Moslem world (one out of seven inhabitants of

the earth) who correctly view Christians as assenting to Jewish atrocities.[42]

What an utterly bizarre claim! The Muslim world has no problem accepting our financial assistance, military backing and modern technology, nor does it hesitate to send us its promising young intellectuals for university training—all in spite of our solidarity with Israel. And of course, the question that is begging to be asked is this: If it is U.S. support for Israel that is frustrating Christian missionary work among the Muslims, what, pray tell, was frustrating Christian missions to the Muslim world in the last century, not to mention the previous 1200 years, when there was no repugnant state of Israel for America to support? And what about non-American Christian missionaries to the Muslims? Why are they having such a hard time too?

Tragically, as preposterous as these anti-Israel statements are, a nationally recognized Bible teacher echoes their sentiment:

> It is hurting our witness to the Arab nations when we sanction anything Israel does. Political Israel is not Israel. They have no right...to be on that land.[43]

But there are quotes far more frightening than anything we might have imagined.

Read these words and tremble:

> The representative view can therefore advocate love for the Jew, while being able to reject his anti-Christian nation that persecutes Christians and butchers other people who need Christ just as much as they. It can work for the conversion of Israel without becoming the pawn of a maniacal nationalism, a racial supremacy as ugly and potentially oppressive as its twentieth century arch enemy, Aryanism [i.e., Nazism!].[44]

Read these words and weep:

> ...we have unearthed irrefutable evidence that Israel is a
> dominant and moving force behind the present and coming
> evils of our day. To our amazement we find that Israel is not
> that trusted, familiar friend we thought we had known.
> Rather she is a misshapen facsimile of everything we had so
> fondly bid godspeed to....We are at last confronted with a
> monstrous system of evil which, if unresisted, will destroy
> us and our children and bring the entire world into such
> darkness, oppression, and satanic dominion that only the
> coming of Jesus Christ can make it right again.[45]

All this from a concerned "Christian" pen! Are there *no*
seeds of anti-Semitism among us?

So, Zionism is as ugly as Nazism, Israel is poised to take
over the world and plunge it into satanic darkness and the
Muslims would get saved if America would only quit backing this miserable little Jewish state—a state that happens
to be the only democracy in the Middle East as well as
America's most loyal ally!

And what about Israel's alleged horrible persecution of
Christians? Try this fact on for size: It was the bigoted,
racist, evil Israelis who strongly opposed the showing of
"The Last Temptation of Christ" in their country. Why?
They didn't want to offend the Christians!

I wonder who the true bigots are...

Chapter Seven

Lies! Lies! Lies!

Many strange tales have been told about the Jewish people, but none is stranger than the tale of the Wandering Jew. According to the legend, as Jesus was on His way to be crucified, a Jewish man either struck or rebuffed the Son of God. As a result of his irreverence, the Lord condemned him to wander the earth until the Second Coming.

Just a harmless legend, right? Not quite. First, countless thousands of people, especially in medieval Europe, actually believed the story. On numerous occasions, people reported meeting the Wandering Jew in person! He was allegedly seen in 1223 by some pilgrims passing through Armenia; he supposedly made an appearance at a church in Germany in 1542 and, according to local traditions, he was also sighted in Luebeck (1603), Paris (1604), Brussels (1640), Leipzig (1642), Munich (1721) and London (1818).

The different names by which he has been known include Ahasuerus, Cartaphilus, Buttadeus, Boutedieu, Votadio and Juan Espera en Dios, to name just a few. The anti-Semitic imagination is quite creative! A famous German book written about this Wandering Jew (based on his supposed church visit in 1542) was translated or paraphrased into French, Danish, Estonian and Italian.[1]

Why all this interest in such an absurd story? It's quite simple. It personified the Church's viewpoint of the Jewish people as a whole. They were guilty as a nation of the crucifixion of Jesus; therefore, they must continually wander around the world, destitute, homeless, persecuted and always suffering, as a constant witness to the truth of the gospel message. The Jews are cursed; the Christians are blessed. That proves that Christianity is right!

Now, the story of the Wandering Jew should show us something Satan has known for a long time. If you tell ridiculous, impossible, hateful and venomous lies; if you tell them long enough and loud enough, especially if they are about the Jews, much of the Church, along with the rest of the world, will believe you.

Adolf Hitler observed that "the great masses of the people...more easily fall victim to a big lie than to a little one." Have *we* fallen victim to any big lies against the Jews?

In 1348-1349 the Black Death ravaged Europe, wiping out about *one-third* of Europe's entire population. Who was to blame? The Jews of course! (The fact that the Black Plague also killed multitudes of Jews didn't seem to bother anyone.) Just how did the Jews execute such a wide-ranging plan of destruction? They secretly contaminated the wells with a poisonous mixture made of spiders, lizards and the hearts of Christians mixed together with the sacred elements of the Lord's Supper.[2]

Hundreds of thousands of "Christians" believed this lie. As a result, thousands of Jews were butchered by angry mobs and "Jewish children under the age of seven were then baptized and reared as Christians after their families were murdered."[3] What was the "proof" that the Jews were guilty? Some of them "confessed" to the crime—under severe torture. Otherwise, no "evidence" existed.

Then there was the charge of "desecrating the host":

In 1215, the Fourth Lateran Council accepted the doctrine of transubstantiation as official Church dogma. This dogma asserted that the wafer used at the Mass was miraculously transformed into the body of Jesus.…[This] belief in the doctrine of transubstantiation led to the torture and murder of thousands of Jews. Since Jesus is brought to life through the wafer, would not the Jews who had once crucified him wish to torture and kill him again? In 1243…[Berlin's] entire Jewish community was burned alive for allegedly torturing a wafer.…In Prague, in 1389, the Jewish community was collectively accused of attacking a monk carrying a wafer. Large mobs of Christians surrounded the Jewish neighborhood and offered the Jews the choice of baptism or death. Refusing to be baptized, three thousand Jews were murdered. In Berlin, in 1510, twenty-six Jews were burned and two beheaded for reportedly "desecrating the host." A charge of host desecration was reported as late as 1836 in Romania.[4]

Probably the most widespread anti-Jewish lie that has been told, and believed, through the ages has been the charge of ritual murder.[5] The story is always the same: A group of Jews kidnap a Christian child (often before Easter), torture him, kill him (often by crucifixion) and more times than not, drink the blood. The remaining blood is also put to good use: The Jews use it for making Passover matzoh (unleavened bread)! As expected, the only "evidence" for the crime is always the same: Jews under torture "confess."

This is a typical account:

> April 26, 1343. A ritual murder accusation is raised against the Jews of Germersheim, Germany. Thereupon, the town's whole Jewish community is burned at the stake.[6]

God only knows how many Jews lost their lives because of this infamous blood libel. The numbers are surely in the multiplied tens of thousands. And God only knows how many people—Muslim, Atheist and "Christian"—believe this lie today. *It has been circulating for over 2000 years.* In its earliest "non-Christian" form, it was spread by the Greeks and Romans.[7] It has made its way across the world: A ballad inspired by this Jewish blood libel was recently found in a book of folk songs in the Ozark Mountains of Arkansas,[8] while a booklet published in Birmingham, Alabama in 1962 gave credence to the charge of Jewish ritual murder.[9]

Just consider these sickening facts. According to Church historian James Parkes:

> In Central Eastern Europe, among both Roman Catholics and Eastern Orthodox Christians...there are almost more examples of the accusation [of ritual murder] between 1880 and 1945 than in the whole of the Middle Ages.[10]

The blood libel was also utilized by the Nazis.

The entire May 1, 1934, issue of the Nazi newspaper *Der Stuermer* was devoted to Jewish ritual murder, and the regular weekly edition of the paper routinely carried illustrations of rabbis sucking the blood of German children.

In the 1960s and the 1970s the blood libel was spread by the leading financial figure in the Arab world, the late King Faisal of Saudi Arabia. On a number of occasions Faisal informed newspaper interviewers that the Jews annually celebrated Passover by murdering a non-Jew and consuming his blood.[11]

More recently, Mustafa Tlas, the Defense Minister and Deputy Prime Minister of Syria, wrote a book entitled *The Matzah of Zion*, reviving

a tale concerning Jews in Damascus in 1840 who are said to have killed two Christians to use their blood to make matzah. *The book has been translated into German and was adapted for Kuwaiti television.*[12]

The cancer continues to spread. During a meeting of the U.N. Human Rights Commission held in Geneva on February 8, 1990, Nabila Shaalan, the second-ranking member of the Syrian delegation, urged that *The Matzah of Zion* be read by the other members of the Commission. She called it "a valuable book which confirms the racist character of Zion." No one on the panel rebuffed her for the suggestion.[13]

Here are more lies, some even more grotesque, that you are likely to hear:

The Holocaust never happened! It is merely a Zionist fabrication designed to influence world opinion.[14]

Could there possibly be any lie uglier than that one? And yet, in spite of volumes of indisputable documentary evidence (including actual film footage) and the testimony of tens of thousands of eye-witnesses, many of whom are still alive today, there are "learned" books being written, including university dissertations, seeking to deny the Holocaust.

This tragic deception is spreading throughout Europe, the Middle East, the Far East, Africa, South America and North America. (In other words, it's spreading everywhere.)

One evangelical author in the United States seems to give credence to the view that the commonly accepted number of Jewish casualties in the Holocaust (i.e., 6,000,000) is a wild exaggeration.[15] A bishop of the recently formed traditionalist Catholic Church in Quebec stated that the Holocaust "may be a very big lie."[16] These concerned "Christian" men may have never read works written by Holocaust survivors. Many times the book dedications begin with words like these: "In memory of my grandmother, my father, my mother, my wife, my two daughters (aged eleven and eight), and my three sons (aged fourteen, six and four). Killed by the Nazis, 1943." If only it had been an exaggeration or a very big lie![17]

The Jews control all the banks and all the money. They are responsible for the entire world's economic problems.[18]

Aside from the fact that the Jewish people make up less than .003% of the world's population (13 million out of 5.5 billion) and that they certainly do not control the vast amounts of *Arab* money flowing from oil rich nations in the Gulf, hardly any Jews even *live* in some of the countries where they are being accused. To give just one glaring example, several best-selling books in *Japan* blame that country's economic problems on the Jews. The fact that most Japanese people have never met a Jew in their lives (less than *1000* Jews live in Japan) has not stopped this dangerous fabrication from infecting public opinion. It even has political support: *The Secret of Jewish Power to Control the World* was written by Aisaburo Saito, a member of the Japanese legislature.[19]

> *The Jews are working secretly with the Communists (or, with the Fascists, or, with the Socialists—whomever we don't like at the moment).*[20]

According to this nonsense, the Kremlin and the Knesset are in cahoots! Too bad for the Jews that, while they covertly dominate world politics, they are always getting overtly persecuted and butchered by the nations they supposedly manipulate! Too bad for the Jews that, while they control the international television and press, they are always getting bashed by the media! Too bad for the Jews that, while they *do* have many influential people in high places, they are totally divided into opposing factions and conflicting ideologies! There are leading Jews on the left and leading Jews on the right. So much for a world conspiracy! But let's be realistic. If people can believe that the Jews are responsible for the Black Death and guilty of using Christian blood in their unleavened bread, they can believe this world domination rubbish too!

It should not surprise us, then, that *The Protocols of the Elders of Zion* (a complete fabrication judged by scholars to be "ridiculous nonsense" and "immoral") has become very popular again. This book, a big favorite of anti-Semites for the last century, really sets the record straight: 300 secret Jewish kings will conquer the world and bring all humanity under the influence of the Hindu god Vishnu! People are actually reading this book *today.* And they are believing what it says! In fact, according to a recent report, both *The Protocols of the Elders of Zion* and Hitler's *Mein Kampf* have been recommended as must reading for all members of Russia's Red Army.[21]

> *Today's Jews are not really Jews. They are actually Europeans who converted to Judaism. (Further variations on this notion include the belief that the original Jews were all black.)*[22]

Somehow, this amazing piece of information has eluded the world's greatest historians for centuries, not to mention that it raises some fairly serious questions. In the last fifteen hundred years, when was conversion to Judaism the "in thing"? When did it become so popular to be Jewish? Yet, if most of today's Jews, including virtually *all* of the Ashkenazi Jews, are converts, then conversion to Judaism must have been rampant for decades! And why was it that during times of anti-Semitic persecution these Jews forgot they weren't originally Jewish after all? *Hitler forgot too.* The European Jews were slaughtered during the Nazi era *solely because they were ethnically Jewish;* conversion or assimilation wouldn't help. Yet some people would have us believe they weren't actually Jewish!

There are writers today who allude to the conversion of the Khazars in the eighth century, claiming that most European Jews can be traced back to them.[23] Of course, if many of them did truly convert, then God would have accepted them as Jews, just as He accepted Ruth. (A Jew is anyone born of Jewish parents or anyone who identifies himself with the Jewish people through conversion.) But history tells us that the conversion of the Khazars to Judaism was *not* perfect and complete, that only a small number of them actually trickled into the general European Jewish community (most of the conversions were limited to the royal family), and that by the fourteenth century these Khazar converts had practically disappeared. Some of those who converted to Judaism later converted to Christianity or Islam![24]

And what happened to the "real Jews," the ones who allegedly converted the converts? Were they actually black Jews who secretly infiltrated Europe (like stealth bombers, undetected by all historical records), converted masses of Gentiles and then vanished from existence? What a bizarre proposition!

But it doesn't stop there. According to this theory, there was vast intermarriage between Jews and Gentiles—with the Gentiles assimilating into Jewish society. This is the exact opposite of what normally happens when Jews intermarry with Gentiles. It is the *Jews* who assimilate into Gentile society. Of course, historians tell us that some Gentiles have entered Jewish society through conversion and intermarriage, but the percentages are incredibly low.[25]

Yet why should historical truth get in the way of a big lie? This notion that "today's Jews are not the true Jews" serves a useful purpose. It allows someone like Louis Farrakhan to despise European and American Jews while denying that he is anti-Semitic since in his eyes, these Jews aren't Semitic![26] Too bad that Richard Wagner, the nineteenth century German opera composer, didn't know the facts. He complained:

> Culture was unsuccessful in eradicating the peculiar stubbornness of the Jewish nature with respect of the characteristics of the Semitic manner of expression despite two thousand years of intercourse with European nations.[27]

In other words, civilized Europe couldn't cure the Jews of their coarse Semitic nature! Once again, the Jews are damned if they do and damned if they don't. They are either at fault because they *are* Semitic or they are at fault because they are *not* Semitic.

In every generation, Satan has sought to destroy the Jewish people through *assimilation.* In the last generation, he added a new weapon to his arsenal: *extermination.* Since that failed and he couldn't completely get rid of them, he decided to try something new: *disinformation.* The Jews are not really Jews! How clever of the devil. Since he can't wipe the Jewish people out, he'll just claim that they're not really here.

> *The Talmud not only condones child molestation, bestiality and other forms of immorality, it actually sanctions them.*[28]

Aside from the fact that neither Jesus nor the apostles ever charged even the worst of Jewish leadership with such sins, Jewish history testifies to the exact opposite of this groundless slander. It is universally recognized that observant Jewish communities have an extraordinarily *low* rate of crime, sexual immorality and perversion.[29] Yet these well known facts have not stopped some recent Christian authors from completely twisting the words of the Talmud, taking quotes entirely out of context and presenting the Talmudic rabbis as perverts. (By the way, if you want to understand what the Talmud says, you should ask a rabbi, not someone filled with anti-Jewish sentiments.) It is also strange that these same rabbis can be accused of being strict legalists in one breath, while in the next breath they are accused of being sensual libertarians!

But there is an ultimate lie that is even worse. A widely distributed Christian video says that the medieval Church persecuted the religious Jews because these highly moral (!) Christians were offended by the sexual perversions of the degenerate Jews.[30] What a demonic fabrication! It is not the rabbis who were perverse, it is this rewriting of history that is perverse.

> *The Arab nations are all peace loving. Their only gripe with the Jews came when the imperialistic Zionists stole their land in 1948. In fact, those Jews are occupying stolen land today!*[31]

For the moment let's ignore the fact that God Almighty promised the Land to His people Israel *for ever.* (If you don't believe this, maybe you've swallowed a lie here too. If you have some honest questions, keep reading. We'll come back to this biblical issue later.)

Did the Jews really steal Arab land? Were their sins against the Arabs even greater than America's sins against its native Indian population? Are the Zionists the ones primarily responsible for displacing the Palestinians?

Michael Comay points out that in 1948, just before the British withdrawal from Palestine began, 9% of the land was owned by Jews, 3% by Arab national citizens living in the Land,

> 17% was abandoned Arab land and the remaining 71% was Crown or State Land vested in the Mandatory [British] Government and subsequently in the State of Israel."[32]

Although the Jewish people, newly settled in their ancient homeland, cautiously accepted the U.N. defined borders—borders essentially indefensible—they were attacked by five neighboring Arab states the very day Israel announced its independence.[33]

Surrounding Arab nations committed the first acts of war in 1948, 1956, 1967 and 1973, and the PLO struck first before Israel's invasion of Lebanon in 1982.[34] It was more than thirty years before Egypt became the first neighboring Arab country to sign a peace treaty with Israel. In other words, the other Arab nations remained in a state of declared war with Israel continually, not even recognizing Israel's right to *exist*. (Think of being surrounded by that 24 hours a day!) Rather than stay in the Land and live together with the Jews, tens of thousands of Arabs chose to flee for a short time and return after their brothers drove the Jews out. Their goals are still the same.

Professor David Rausch notes:

> On many occasions [in 1948] the Arab High Command
> declared to the Palestinians: "A cannon cannot differentiate
> between a Jew and an Arab. Leave the country for two
> weeks and you will come back victorious."[35]

More than forty years later, these nationless Palestinians
are still waiting for Arab victory over the Jewish state. All
Palestinian liberation groups—Fatah, Saika, the PLF, the
PLFP, the PLFP-GC, the DFLP *and the PLO*—have stated
their aims clearly: The formation of a Palestinian state is
only the first step toward driving the Jews completely out
of the Land.[36] It is these very groups who have provoked
and publicized the Intifada.

This does not mean that all Arabs are war-mongers or
that all Israelis are doves. But Israel does *not* relish spend-
ing more than 20% of its tightly strained budget on defense.
Who would? The U.S.S.R., which exported its military
goods around the world, spent only 15% of its budget on
"defense"; the U.S.A. currently spends only 6%.

And let's not forget what Israel has done *on behalf* of
their land. For centuries the land of Palestine was largely a
swamp-filled, untilled waste. But Jewish pioneers drained
the malaria-infested swamps—often at the cost of their
lives—and made the land into what it is today: an agricul-
tural delight![37] Has anyone thanked the Jewish people for
that?

As for the question of a Palestinian state, believers need
to hear the truth so they can pray and act truthfully. If *we*
don't take a stand for righteousness, who will? Here are
some things we should know: It is a fact that Israel accepted

the U.N. partitioning of the Land in 1948 into an Israeli state and a Palestinian state; the Arab nations did not. It is a fact that the so-called West Bank (Judea and Samaria) and Gaza were under the control of Jordan and Egypt until 1967. Neither country made any effort to form a Palestinian state for the refugees. It is a fact that the Arab nations are able to absorb the Palestinians into their own lands, but they have made absolutely no effort to do so.

The Palestinian refugee problem simply does not have to continue. After the establishment of Israel, 800,000 Jews left Arab lands, compared with 600,000 Palestinian Arabs who left Israel for Arab lands. These Jews left behind property valued at five times the amount of Arab refugees' property in Israel. The Jewish state, 640 times *smaller* than the Arab world and only one-fiftieth of its population, successfully absorbed most of its Jewish refugees.[38] Why haven't the Arab nations absorbed the Palestinians? Why have some of these nations spent hundreds of millions of dollars funding Palestinian terrorist activity and only tens of millions (at best) on Palestinian humanitarian aid?

Ralph Galloway, former head of the United Nations Relief and Works Agency for Palestinian Refugees, writes:

> The Arab States do not want to solve the refugee problem. They want to keep it as an open sore, as an affront to the United Nations and as a weapon against Israel. Arab leaders don't care whether the refugees live or die.[39]

In fact, some Palestinians

> say bluntly that Israel treats them better than anyone in this region. "At least they won't bother you unless you bother them," says Hanifi Younes [a Palestinian living in

Kuwait]...“Their democratic ideals protect us. But in Arab countries, they’ll mistreat us as lower life forms.”[40]

Under Israeli control, the quality of life for the Palestinians living in the so-called Occupied Territories (Judea/Samaria and the Gaza District) has greatly improved. Life expectancy has increased from 48 years to 62 years; infant mortality has dropped sharply (especially in Judea/Samaria); overcrowding has been reduced, and even modern conveniences are much more readily available. To give just two examples, in 1967 only 3% of those in the Gaza District had refrigerators or cooking ranges; by the mid 1980’s, 77% had refrigerators and 87% had cooking ranges.[41]

As for the tiny Jewish state’s so-called agressive expansionism, the fact is that Israel has *returned* 91% of the land it occupied as a result of the Six Day War.[42] Although some claim that there would be peace in the Middle East if only Israel would surrender *more* territory (the “land for peace” concept), the sad truth is that Arabs have been *killing each other* for decades, without any reference to Israel. In fact, the Arab nations have not even been unified *since* Israel became a state.

The history of the Arab world since 1948 is marked by murder, subversion, coup d’etats, persecutions, civil wars, hatred and bloodshed. Hundreds of thousands of Arabs were murdered by fellow Arabs. Many hundreds of leaders, presidents, kings, ministers, religious leaders and other dignitaries were assassinated. At different times, the Arab armies fought one another and caused tens of thousands of casualties.[43]

Even Abd Alhalim Khaddam, the Syrian Foreign Minister, admitted in 1980:

> If we look at a map of the Arab Homeland, we can hardly find two countries without conflict...We can hardly find two countries which are not either in a state of war or on the road to war.[44]

And Jordan's King Hussein, speaking of the civil war in Lebanon which took scores of thousands of Arab lives, remarked:

> It can now be seen that Arabs themselves, citizens of the same country, not only cannot coexist but collide day and night.[45]

Saddam Hussein's invasion of Kuwait and Syria's aggression in Lebanon are the most recent examples of internal Arab strife. Most conflicts in the region are not even *related* to Arab-Jew disputes.

But who cares about reality anyway? Lies about Israel make for much better press! So the list of lies goes on and on. In the last decade Steve Cokely, an aide to the mayor of Chicago, accused Jewish doctors of injecting the AIDS virus into Blacks,[46] while a tract circulating in some French high schools accused "Israeli mercenaries" of giving AIDS to young French women. In Russia, a nationalist writer alleged that Jews (and Masons) were preparing Russian children for a life of debauchery by regularly feeding them yogurt with an alcohol content of at least 1.5%, and in Mexico, a neo-Nazi group claimed that Jews were seeking worldwide spiritual domination by infiltrating "Jewish priests and popes into the Catholic Church."[47] Back in the

States, a congressional candidate in New Jersey said that efforts of the U.S. Justice Department aimed against Nazi war criminals are really "persecutions of Christians."[48] What in the world will come next?

No doubt these lies will continue. Satan has found an effective, lethal tool. But there is a simple way *you* can counteract this anti-Jewish venom: The next time someone tells you that the Holocaust never happened, tell him you'll believe it...

after you meet the Wandering Jew.

Chapter Eight

The Inquisition Isn't Over

Everyone has heard about the Spanish Inquisition. In the days of Christopher Columbus and of Ferdinand and Isabella of Spain, the Catholic Church launched a terrible persecution against suspected heretics. Thousands were imprisoned, tortured and burned at the stake.

All this is common knowledge. But how many of us know that there was one particular "heresy" the Spanish Inquisition sought to uncover and destroy? There was a witch hunt against baptized Jews who maintained *any* vestige of Jewishness! These Catholic Jews (called "Marranos," "Conversos" or "New Christians"), violently forced to convert in the first place, were carefully watched to see if they were practicing "heresy." Heretical practices included failure to eat pork; failure to work on Saturday; failure to wear one's best clothes on Sunday; keeping the biblical feasts; observing any Jewish customs of any kind; saying any Jewish prayers; preparing food according to Jewish law; associating with non-baptized Jews; and intermarriage of children of Marrano families with children of other Marrano families.[1]

Violators, or frequently those merely *accused* of being violators, would have their property confiscated. They would be subjected to harsh confinement and horrible torture, leading to mock trials, degradation and often death at the stake. If those sentenced to die would renounce their "heresies" and publicly confess the Faith, then the Church would show them mercy: They would be strangled and *then* put to the flame, burned dead instead of alive!

Spain's sins against the Jewish people are great. Although there were Church Inquisitions throughout Western and Central Europe from the twelfth to the nineteenth centuries, the Inquisitions in Spain took on unusually brutal proportions.

It is estimated that 30,000 Marranos were burned at the stake in Spanish Inquisitions from the fifteenth century until 1808. In addition to this, in 1492, all non-baptized Jews were expelled from the country. Stripped of their possessions, and without any means to defend themselves, the sentence of mass expulsion against these poor souls was virtually a sentence of mass death. Those who "converted" did not fare much better—they were treated as second-class citizens by the other Catholics, and just one wrong move could consign them to the fire.

Baptized Jews who wavered but then wanted to be reconciled to the Church were subjected to an act of penance called the *verguenza* ("shame"). They were

> paraded through the streets, men and women alike, bareheaded, barefooted, and naked to the waist.

The procession was headed by a group of monks, followed by the

> half-naked penitents, cruel physical discomfort being added
> to their mental torture, for the weather was so raw and cold
> that it had been considered expedient to provide them with
> sandals, lest they should have found it impossible to walk.

> They held unlit candles in their hands (indicating that they
> were yet in spiritual darkness), and they were marched
> through the city until they arrived at the Cathedral. A
> chaplain would make the sign of the cross on the foreheads
> of these Jews—many of whom had been prominent citizens
> and respected leaders of their city before the Jew-hate craze
> erupted—and then he would recite these words: "Receive
> the Sign of the Cross which you denied, and which, being
> deluded, you lost."[2]

After this a sermon would be preached, and the sentence
would be announced:

> They were to be whipped in procession on each of the fol-
> lowing six Fridays, being naked to the waist, bareheaded
> and barefooted; they were to fast on each of those six
> Fridays, and they were disqualified for the rest of their lives
> from holding office, benefice, or honourable employment,
> and from using gold, silver, precious stones, or fine fabrics.[3]

When their six-week penance was completed, they had
to give alms "to the extent of one-fifth of the value of their
property."

This was how the "Church" treated those who returned
to the fold![4]

Some Jews who were arrested and tortured still refused
to convert. In the midst of indescribable agony, a Jew
would be told that

...the torments would be terminated if he wholeheartedly accepted Christianity. A fitting response to this temptation was laid down in the course of the fifteenth century:

"The moment of his resolution to Hallow the Name by his martyrdom is when they wish to torture and question him...and they tell him that if he exchanges his honour they will let him alone...Indeed, I have found what one of the pious wrote should be his answer: 'What are you asking of me? Indeed I am a Jew. A Jew I live and a Jew I die. A Jew, Jew, Jew!' "[5]

Many of them died in this way. Whose side do you think God was on? Is it possible that He approved of the methods and dogmas of the apostate Church of that day? Hardly! It was not *His* Spirit that motivated the torturers. Nor was it a victory when the Jews would convert. They simply became members of the Catholic Church without really being introduced to Jesus, since most of the clergy didn't know Him either!

The Jews of Spain (along with many other Jews in many other lands in many other centuries) were brutally squeezed between a rock and a hard place. God wanted them to hear the gospel and be saved. Yet the Church was not preaching the gospel! God wanted them to be Jews who followed Jesus. But the Church said, "Either Jesus or Jewish!" God wanted them to live and die as Jews who knew the Messiah. But the Church made that impossible. If a Jew wanted to live and die as a Jew, he had to deny the Messiah; if he wanted to know the Messiah (or, at least, the Messiah the Church presented), he could no longer be a Jew.

The Judaism of that day did not know Jesus the Messiah. The Church of that day failed to reveal Him. What was a Jew to do? His future was bleak. He could only look forward to expulsion, torture, humiliation, servitude or conversion to a lifeless religion. The Church, at least, that which called itself the Church, was steeped in darkness. Its cloud enveloped the Jews.

As far as history is concerned, the Inquisitions ended more than one hundred years ago. But the spirit of the Inquisitions lives on. There is still a passionate desire to rid the Church, especially its Jewish believers, of all Jewishness—even though the Messiah is a Jew! (Some believers would be happy if they could strip *Yeshua Himself* of His Jewishness. Theologians under Hitler tried to do this very thing, arguing in their books that Jesus was actually an Aryan, not a Jew. Even a prominent German New Testament scholar like Walter Grundmann—he continued to publish influential studies for many years after the end of the Hitler regime—wrote a book in 1940 in which "he attempted to show that Jesus, being mentally and pyschologically completely un-Jewish, must have been the same even biologically and physically."[6] Some people are more at home with a blond-haired, blue-eyed, European Jesus, than with Yeshua, a Middle Eastern Jew!)

I understand fully that in the Lord, all believers, both Jewish and Gentile, are free from *bondage* to the Law. Jesus is our justification, our righteousness and the Perfecter of our faith. We must begin in the Spirit and continue in the Spirit. We can't add anything to that. But what does this have to do with leading a biblical Jewish life? Where does the Word say to Jewish believers, "If you want to follow the Lord, you must abandon your people and your Law?" Is this really a biblical position?

Let's go back to the Gospels. Jesus did not come to abolish the Law and the Prophets, but to fulfill them (Matt. 5:17- 20).[7] He didn't do away with the Hebrew Scriptures, He brought them to completion. The images of the Law were the shadow, Jesus is the substance; but the shadow resembles the substance!

What would we think of a presidential candidate who assured his voters that he would only *uphold* the requirements and *fulfill* the goals of the Constitution and never *abolish* our country's customs and laws, yet two years after his election, plunged the country into complete anarchy? Would this be *fulfillment* of the Constitution or *abolition* of the Constitution? It is the same with the Law of God. If Jesus promised to fulfill it but instead abolished it, then He would be a liar and not the Son of God.

Do you know that this is one of the greatest objections to the gospel that religious Jews have had? If Jesus was truly the Messiah, why did He do away with the Law? Historian Jules Isaac notes:

> The Jewish rejection of Christ was triggered by the Christian rejection of the Law....The rejection of the Law was enough: to ask of the Jewish people that they accept this rejection...was like asking them to tear out their heart. History records no example of such a collective suicide.[8]

Many Christians believe that Jesus annulled the Law and in its place He gave us a New Covenant. But that is not what the Scriptures teach. According to the New Covenant, God said:

> I will put My law in their minds and write it in their hearts (Jer. 31:33b).

Rather than taking the Law away from Israel, God promised to put it in their hearts. The New Covenant does not do away with God's Law. Instead, it makes it relevant in a new and living way. This actually should be *attractive* to other Jews![9]

Of course, observance of the Law does not make us more righteous, more loved or more spiritual. Through the cross our sins are forgiven, and the Spirit leads us in paths of life. But where is it written that believers, in particular Jewish believers, are *forbidden* to observe the Law? Are we free to *break* the Law but not free to *keep* the Law? Where it is written that the Spirit always leads us *away* from and *against* the Law?

Let's get more specific: Where do the Scriptures clearly and decisively make Sunday into the Sabbath?[10] (Forget about later Church tradition. What does the Bible say?) Then why are Jewish believers who set aside Saturday for Sabbath worship considered divisive?

Where does *God* say to forget the biblical feasts? Then why are Jewish believers who celebrate the feasts instead of later, man-made holidays accused of going back under the Law?[11]

Where does the *Word* teach that Jews must become Gentiles to be saved? We have really forgotten our roots!

Let's go back to the Book of Acts. The early Church was exclusively Jewish. It was almost *ten years* before a group of Gentiles received the gospel, and this created shock waves in Jerusalem. Some men began to teach these new believers:

Unless you are circumcised, according to the custom taught by Moses, you cannot be saved.

They argued that,

the Gentiles must be circumcised and required to obey the law of Moses (Acts 15:1, 5).

Of course, their position was completely wrong. But there is something important to notice. The question was not whether Jews who followed Jesus were *allowed* to continue obeying the Law. No one ever dreamed of such a question! Jesus had kept the Law, and His disciples sought to keep it too. Instead the question was this: Were Gentiles who followed Jesus *required* to keep the Law?[12]

Look at how much our thinking has changed! In the Book of Acts they wondered whether Gentiles had to become Jews in order to be saved. Today the Church wonders whether Jews can be saved without becoming Gentiles! We say that there is neither Jew nor Gentile in the Body. It's true! We've made it *all* Gentile! We are quick to smell out the Judaizers, and that's good. Judaizing *is* a dangerous tendency that must be avoided. But are we on the lookout for the Gentilizers?

Did you know that many Jewish believers have been served ham sandwiches at church luncheons, to make sure they are "free"? Thank God, no one is burning us at the stake. But it would be nice for us to have a little more understanding.

All of us affirm Peter's words:

> We believe it is through the grace of our Lord Jesus that we
> [Jews] are saved, just as they [Gentiles] are (Acts 15:11).

The works of the Law cannot save—ever. But casting
off the Law doesn't save either! Where is it written that an
anti-Law spirit is virtuous? Where it is written that breaking the food laws is meritorious? Where it is written that
abandoning the commandments brings us closer to God?
Yet this seems to be the position some Christians take.

How did Paul describe Ananias, the disciple who mini-
stered to him after he met the Lord on the road to Damascus?

> A man named Ananias came to see me. He was a devout
> observer of the law and highly respected by all the Jews
> living there (Acts 22:12).

What a tremendous compliment! And Paul spoke these
words toward the end of his life. Certainly *Paul* understood
the doctrine of grace!

James, the Lord's brother, shared with Paul the exciting
news that

> many thousands of Jews have believed, and *all of them are
> zealous for the law* (Acts 21:20).

Paul himself even demonstrated publicly that he did *not*

> teach all the Jews who live among the Gentiles to turn away
> from Moses, telling them not to circumcise their children or
> live according to our customs."

No. He himself was "living in obedience to the law
(Acts 21:21-25).[13]

In the epistles Paul also taught about this clearly. In
Romans he raised an important question: "Do we, then,

nullify the law by this faith?" This was his categorical answer: "Not at all! Rather, we uphold the law" (Rom. 3:31).[14]

In fact, according to Paul:

the law is holy, and the commandment is holy, righteous and good....the law is spiritual (Rom. 7:12, 14).

In First Corinthians Paul stated in no uncertain terms that

Circumcision is nothing and uncircumcision is nothing. Keeping God's commands is what counts (1 Cor. 7:19).

This is just what he said to the Galatians:

Neither circumcision nor uncircumcision means anything; what counts is a new creation....For in Christ Jesus neither circumcision nor uncircumcision has any value. The only thing that counts is faith expressing itself through love (Gal. 6:15; 5:6).

As far as salvation and relating to God is concerned, circumcision carries no weight at all. But Paul also had this to say:

Was a man already circumcised when he was called? He should not become uncircumcised. Was a man uncircumcised when he was called? He should not be circumcised.... Each one should remain in the situation which he was in when God called him (1 Cor. 7:18, 20).

This is pretty clear too! *A Jew who becomes saved should continue to live as a Jew,* just as a man who becomes saved continues to live as a man and a woman who becomes saved continues to live as a woman. The Jew who becomes born from above must cast off all death-giving traditions. He must throw aside all feelings of superiority.

He must put no trust in his heritage. He must enter into new life in the Spirit. He must boast in Jesus and the cross alone. But he should continue to live as a Jew—wherever it does *not* contradict the Word or hinder the Spirit's flow. Paul says plainly that this is right.[15]

And what about Jewish believers specially called to minister to their own people? Listen again to Paul:

> Though I am free and belong to no man, I make myself a slave to everyone, to win as many as possible. To the Jews I became like a Jew, to win the Jews. To those under the law I became like one under the law (though I myself am not under the law), so as to win those under the law (1 Cor. 9:19-20).

He took on Jewish customs *that he did not have to,* and he submitted himself to all kinds of traditional laws *that were not binding* in order to win his fellow Jews.[16] Jewish believers can follow his method here too, as long as we follow his message, preaching the unadulterated, uncompromised gospel with signs, wonders and the power of God.

As for the Gentile believers at Corinth, Paul had an exhortation:

> ...Christ, our Passover lamb, has been sacrificed. *Therefore let us keep the Festival,* not with the old yeast, the yeast of malice and wickedness, but with bread without yeast, the bread of sincerity and truth (1 Cor. 5:7-8).

Every believer can keep Israel's feasts! Jesus has opened the door.

> Consequently, you are no longer foreigners and aliens, but fellow citizens with God's [Jewish] people and members of

God's household, built on the foundation of the apostles and prophets, with Christ Jesus Himself as the chief cornerstone (Eph. 2:19-20).

The wild olive branches (Gentiles) have been grafted into the natural (Israelite) tree. So

do not boast over those [natural] branches. If you do, consider this: You do not support the root, but the root supports you (Rom. 11:17-18).

The Church must thank God for the root!

Let us decisively sever all ties with the sinful prejudices of the Inquisition. It is an inexpressibly disgraceful past.

The Inquisition would have burned Peter and Paul
at the stake.

Chapter Nine

Are You a Crusader for Christ?

According to Romans 11:11, "salvation has come to the Gentiles to make Israel envious." When the Jewish people see that it is the *Gentiles* who have Israel's Messiah, the *Gentiles* who are enjoying the manifest presence of God, the *Gentiles* who are experiencing the covenant blessings, the *Gentiles* who are walking in the joy of the Lord, then Israel will become envious. But has the Church made Israel envious?

Let me translate for you the words of an Israeli writer who expresses the heart of many of his people:

Instead of bringing redemption to the Jews, the false Christian messiah has brought down on us base libels and expulsions, oppressive restrictions and burning of [our] holy books, devastations and destructions. Christianity, which professes to infuse the sick world with love and compassion, has fixed a course directly opposed to this lofty rhetoric. The voice of the blood of millions of our brothers cries out to us from the ground: "No! Christianity is not a religion of love

but a religion of unfathomable hate! All history, from ancient times to our own day, is one continuous proof of the
total bankruptcy of this religion in all its segments."[1]

Rabbi Ephraim Oshry, one of the few Lithuanian rabbis
who survived the Holocaust, wrote:

Another shocking surprise for us was the position taken by
the Lithuanian populace—our "good" Christian neighbors.
There was literally not one gentile among the Christians of
Slobodka who openly defended a Jew at a time when
Slobodka's ten thousand Jews, with whom they had lived
together all their lives, were threatened with the most horrible pogrom imaginable.[2]

On the evening of June 25, 1941, the Lithuanian fascists
began

going from house to house, from apartment to apartment,
murdering people by the most horrible deaths—men,
women, and children—old and young. They hacked off
heads, sawed people through like lumber, prolonging the
agony of their victims as long as possible.[3]

Finding the Rabbi of Slobodka studying Talmud in his
home, they "bound him to a chair, put his head on his open
[Talmud volume] and sawed his head off"—before
slaughtering the rest of his family.

Yet, while the crazed Lithuanians raised their weapons
to destroy the Jews, the "Christian" Lithuanians hardly
raised a finger to defend them.

Professor Eugene Borowitz explains:

We might be more inclined to give Christian claims some
credence had we seen Christians through the ages behave as
models of a redeemed humanity. Looking through the window of history we have found them in as much need of

saving as the rest of humankind. If anything, their social failings are especially discrediting of their doctrine for they claim to be uniquely free of human sinfulness and freshly inspired by their faith to bring the world to a realm of love and peace....Until sinfulness ceases and well-being prevails, Jews know the Messiah has not come.[4]

The fact that a leading Jewish thinker like Eliezer Berkovits could speak of "the moral bankruptcy of Christian civilization and the spiritual bankruptcy of Christian religion"[5] should cut us to the heart.

Berkovits goes on to say:

After nineteen centuries of Christianity, the extermination of six million Jews, among them one-and-a-half million children, carried out in cold blood in the very heart of Christian Europe, encouraged by the criminal silence of virtually all Christendom, including that of an infallible Holy Father in Rome, was the natural culmination of this bankruptcy. A straight line leads from the first act of oppression against the Jews and Judaism in the fourth century to the holocaust in the twentieth.[6]

For hundreds of years, "Christ" has been a curse word in thousands of Jewish homes. This is largely the fault of "Christians." Millions of Jews have hated the name of Jesus. Alleged followers of Jesus are a primary cause. Could we possibly have produced anything worse?

Two thousand years ago, the cross brought reproach because it represented the ultimate scandal to the Jews: The Messiah died a criminal's death! For the last 1500 years, the cross has brought reproach because of a different scandal: The Church has often led a criminal life! Franz Delitzsch, the brilliant Old Testament scholar, noted:

> The Church still owes the Jews the actual proof of
> Christianity's truth. Is it surprising that the Jewish people
> are such an insensitive and barren field for the Gospel? The
> Church itself has drenched it in blood and then heaped
> stones upon it.[7]

This is not meant to whitewash the Jewish people or to
say that they bear no responsibility for rejecting Jesus. The
sad fact is that most Jews were never directly exposed to
Him. Most of them never heard the real gospel. In the
words of Nicolai Berdyaev:

> Christians set themselves between the Messiah and the
> Jews, hiding from the latter the authentic image of the
> Savior.[8]

This is *not* what our Father desired!

Consider the Holy Crusades for Christ. In the eleventh,
twelfth and thirteenth centuries, the Church launched
military expeditions aimed at emancipating the Holy Land
from the Muslims. European Christians had become concerned when they heard that pilgrims were being
mistreated and even barred from the Holy Sites. As a result,
large, often fanatical, "Christian" armies were organized,
sometimes at the bidding of the Pope, sometimes by the
will of the masses. A rabid zeal for the glory of the Church
was fanned into flame—and both Muslim and Jewish "un-
believers" were marked.[9]

Three major Crusades were carried out, and each time
the story was the same: As the impassioned armies marched
through Europe and the Middle East, they committed
atrocities against the Jews. On one occasion they set a
synagogue on fire and then marched around it singing

"Christ We Adore Thee" while the Jews burned to death within.[10]

This has left an indelible impression on the minds of the Jewish people: *The Crusaders affixed crosses to their outer garments.* To Jews who know their past, crusade and cross are dirty words.

Here are some examples of the horrors that took place, in spite of sporadic government intervention (always for a substantial fee!) and occasional Church protection:

May 3, 1096, Germany. The crusaders surrounded the synagogue of Speyer; unable to break into it, they attacked any Jews they could find outside the synagogue, killing eleven of them. One of the victims, a woman, preferring death to conversion, the only choice left open by the crusaders, inaugurated the tradition of freely accepted martyrdom.[11]

July, 15, 1099, Jerusalem. The city was captured on July 15…where [the Jewish] inhabitants defended themselves alongside their Muslim neighbors, finally seeking refuge in the synagogues which were set on fire by the attackers. A terrible massacre ensued; the survivors were sold as slaves…[and] the Jewish community of Jerusalem came to an end and was not reconstituted for many years.…[12]

March 16-17, 1190, England. The worst outrage took place in York, where a number of local nobles, in heavy debt to the Jews, seized the opportunity to rid themselves of their burden. When attacked, the Jews took refuge in the Castle Keep, which the guard had opened for them; those who remained in the town were slaughtered. On their refusal to allow access to the keep, the Jews were besieged. On March 16, on the eve of Passover, the rabbi Yom Tov b[en] Isaac of Joiny, realizing that all hope was lost, asked his brethren to choose suicide rather than submit to baptism. First setting fire to their possessions, one after the other killed himself. More than 150 died in this way, and the few survivors [who were willing to accept baptism!] were murdered by the mob, who also destroyed the register of debts to the Jews.[13]

All this was considered fitting punishment for the Jews, "the murderers of Christ," "those who had crucified Jesus." The Crusaders were only avenging His death. Hundreds of entire Jewish communities were destroyed by these roving mobs armed with crucifixes and swords.

Naturally, some Jews did convert under pressure. But when the pressure let up and the persecutions seemed to be over, they thought they could safely return to Judaism. They were dead wrong. *After the Crusades came the Inquisitions.*

"Baptism" also has been a dirty word for the Jews, and not only because it symbolized faith in Jesus. It meant much more than that. It meant total apostasy from Judaism and complete betrayal of the Jewish people. In the eyes of the Jewish community, any of their people who became Christians were traitors of the worst kind. Even in Nazi Europe, rabbis would not allow Jews to obtain so much as baptismal *certificates* in order to hide their identity and save their lives.

In the words of Rabbi Oshry:

A baptismal certificate has only one connotation: that the owner of the certificate has, G-d forbid, forsaken his Creator and denied his people, the people G-d chose as His treasure.[14]

In light of this, many of us today who are Jewish followers of Jesus emphasize strongly that we are *still* Jews. We have not forsaken our people or forgotten our history!

As Jewish believers, we sometimes call ourselves "*Messianic* Jews" instead of "Hebrew *Christians*" (Messianic and Christian are synonymous terms). We do this because we don't want our people to stumble over negative terms and misunderstood expressions. If they must stumble, let them stumble over Jesus Himself! We want our people to be confronted with the *person of Jesus,* not with persecutions by the Church. We want them to deal with the *message* of the cross, not with its misuse. We don't even like to use the word "convert." To the Jewish mind this means joining an alien religion, *not* becoming born-again, repentant followers of the Messiah.[15]

Here are some excerpts from typical professions of faith that a Jewish baptismal candidate would have to confess. When you read these paragraphs you will understand what I'm talking about. Our forefathers who converted to Catholicism were required to say words like these:

> I do here and now renounce every rite and observance of the Jewish religion, detesting all its most solemn ceremonies and tenets that in former days I kept and held. In the future I will practise no rite or celebration connected with it, nor any custom of my past error, promising neither to seek it out or perform it....I promise that I will never return to the vomit of Jewish superstition. Never again will I fulfill any of the offices of Jewish ceremonies to which I was addicted, nor ever more hold them dear. [I will] shun all intercourse with other Jews and have the circle of my friends only among other Christians.[16]

> [We will not] associate with the accursed Jews who remain unbaptized....We will not practise carnal circumcision, or celebrate the Passover, the Sabbath or the other feast days

connected with the Jewish religion....With regard to swine's flesh we promise to observe this rule, that if through long custom we are hardly able to eat it, we shall not through fastidiousness or error refuse the things that are cooked with it....And if in all the matters touched on above we are found in any way to transgress...[then] whoever of us is found to transgress shall either perish by the hands of our fellows, by burning or stoning, or [if our lives are spared], we shall at once lose our liberty and you shall give us along with all our property to whomever you please into perpetual slavery...[17]

I renounce the whole worship of the Hebrews, circumcision, all its legalisms, unleavened bread, Passover, the sacrificing of lambs, the feast of Weeks, Jubilees, Trumpets, Atonement, Tabernacles, and all other Hebrew feasts, their sacrifices, prayers, aspersions, purifications, expiations, fasts, Sabbaths, new moons, foods and drinks. And I absolutely renounce every custom and institution of the Jewish laws....in one word, I renounce absolutely everything Jewish...[18]

Together with the ancients, I anathematise also the Chief Rabbis and new evil doctors of the Jews...And I believe and profess the Blessed Virgin Mary, who bore Him according to the flesh, and who remained a virgin, to be truly and actually the Mother of God, and I venerate and honour her truly as the Mother of God Incarnate, and as the Lady and mistress of all creation.[19]

If I wander from the straight path in any way and defile the holy Faith, and try to observe any rites of the Jewish sect, or if I shall delude you in any way in the swearing of this oath...then may all the curses of the law fall upon me...May there fall upon me and upon my house and all my children all the plagues which smote Egypt, and to the horror of others may I suffer in addition the fate of Dathan and Abiram, so that the earth shall swallow me alive, and after

I am deprived of this life I shall be handed over to the eternal fire, in the company of the Devil and his Angels, sharing with the dwellers in Sodom and with Judas the punishment of burning; and when I arrive before the tribunal of the fearful and glorious Judge, our Lord Jesus Christ, may I be numbered in that company to whom the glorious and terrible Judge with threatening mien will say, "Depart from Me, evil-doers, into the eternal fire that is prepared for the Devil and his Angels."[20]

Let us hang our heads in shame.
The "Church" has blood on her hands.

Chapter Ten

"More Tears"

A little more than 100 years ago, a Christian minister to the Jews "was asked what he thought wanting on the part of the friends of Israel. He replied, 'More tears.' "[1]

"More tears" is the urgent need on behalf of the Jewish people and the State of Israel today. "More tears" must flow from the Church's eyes before tears of repentance, and then tears of joy, will flow from Israel's eyes. God grant us more tears!

We must weep and lament because of the sins of our "Christian" forefathers against the Jewish people. But we must also weep for the Jewish people themselves; they are like sheep without a shepherd.

> Jews have been expelled from nearly every country in which they have resided....In nearly every country where [they] have lived, they have at some time been subjected to beatings, torture, and murder, solely because they were Jews.[2]

And now Israel, the only Jewish homeland, is surrounded by hostile armies and besieged by the negative opinions of the world.

We need more tears for the Jewish people because most Jews today are *secular.* (This is especially true of *Israeli* Jews!) They serve the gods of materialism and live for this world alone. They have forgotten the eternal covenant with Abraham; God's voice from Sinai no longer thunders in their ears. There are successful Jewish doctors, lawyers, musicians, movie-makers and businessmen—*ad infinitum* —but their success is almost all natural, not spiritual. That is not primarily what they were created for! God wanted Israel to be a people after His own heart.

We need more tears for the Jewish people because Jews have greatly shaped the world, but hardly according to the Father's plan. Karl Marx, Sigmund Freud and Albert Einstein were all Jews *ethnically.* No three men have had a more far-reaching impact on modern society than these men. Yet God's purpose for Israel was to be a *light* to this world, to declare His righteousness to the nations. The efforts of Marx, Freud and Einstein, as well as those of a host of other influential Jews, have hardly been to the glory of God! The overwhelming majority of Jews alive today have lost sight of their destiny and call.

We need more tears for the Jewish people because the devil has laid a snare at their feet. Tens of thousands of young Jewish men and women have been lured into the cults.[3] What a tragedy that these covenant children, filled with promise and potential, have been enlisted in the ranks of Hare Krishna and Reverend Moon! And a disproportionately high number of Jews have fallen into the occult. God knows, we need more tears.

As Jesus made His triumphal entry into Jerusalem, "the whole crowd of disciples began joyfully to praise God in loud voices for all the miracles they had seen" (Luke 19:37).

But Jesus had other things on His mind.

As He approached Jerusalem and saw the city, He wept over it and said, "If you, even you, had only known on this day what would bring you peace—but now it is hidden from your eyes. The days will come upon you when your enemies will build an embankment against you and encircle you and hem you in on every side. They will dash you to the ground, you and the children within your walls. They will not leave one stone on another, because you did not recognize the time of God's coming to you" (Luke 19:41-44).

Just a few days later, as Jesus made His way to the crucifixion site

A large number of people followed Him, including women who mourned and wailed for Him. Jesus turned and said to them, "Daughters of Jerusalem, do not weep for Me; weep for yourselves and for your children. For the time will come when you will say, 'Blessed are the barren women, the wombs that never bore and the breasts that never nursed!' " (Luke 23:28-29).[4]

Jesus tells us to weep too. There is more bloodshed and destruction in the future for our Jewish people. There is trouble and pain in store for Jerusalem. Whether or not the Jewish people are guilty of sin, whether or not their sufferings are the result of divine judgments, God calls us to weep for them—and with them—just the same.

But the Church's want of tears for Israel has not only hurt the Jewish people; it has also injured Christians. An unchecked cancer has been spreading through our ranks, a disease called "lack of compassion." Deep, repentant love is the only cure.

Amos told the complacent, well-fed leaders of his day that they would be "among the first to go into exile"; that their "feasting and lounging will end" (Amos 6:7). It was because they did not "grieve over the ruin of Joseph," they did not feel their people's pain (Amos 6:6). They were too prosperous, too satisfied, too "blessed" to care about the suffering and deprivation of their brothers. And so the party ended suddenly for them. They were taken captive and never released.

This depicts the Church so well! It is not the persecuted Church that has persecuted the Jews, but the prosperous Church that has hounded them. It is not the humble, broken Church that has robbed God's promises from the Jews, but the arrogant, self-sufficient Church that has stolen them. The Church in its grandeur, the Church in its might, has not "grieved over the ruin of Joseph." It has not felt Israel's anguish. Instead, it has mocked the suffering of the Jewish people. In fact, it has *contributed greatly* to their endless nightmare of pain.

The Church will be healthy only when it grieves for the Jewish people. The Jewish people have suffered because of their sins against God. And the Jewish people have suffered because of mankind's sins against them. For *all* this suffering, the Church must grieve.

Did the Jewish people sin in Jesus' day? That didn't stop the Son of God from weeping! Did the Jewish people sin in Jeremiah's day? That didn't stop the prophet from weeping!

> Oh, that my head were a spring of water and my eyes a fountain of tears! I would weep day and night for the slain of my people (Jer. 9:1).

Even if they refused to repent, the prophet lamented still:

> But if you do not listen, I will weep in secret because of your pride; my eyes will weep bitterly, overflowing with tears, because the LORD's flock will be taken captive (Jer. 13:17).

Isaiah wept when he prophesied destruction over Moab and Babylon, enemies of Judah and Israel. He wept for his own people, too.

> ...Turn away from me; let me weep bitterly. Do not try to console me over the destruction of my people (Is. 22:4).

Jerusalem was about to fall.

In Hebrews we read:

> During the days of Jesus' life on earth, He offered up prayers and petitions with loud cries and tears... (Heb. 5:7).

Now, in heaven, "He always lives to intercede" (Heb. 7:25). Do you think His tears flow today?

Jesus still weeps over Jerusalem. It is hard to understand how children of God who claim to know His voice so well never seem to hear Him cry.

Under the terms of the covenant, *God Himself* brought judgment on Israel. But He still felt His people's pain. After the Babylonians devastated Jerusalem, the Lord said, "*I am grieved over the disaster I have inflicted on you*" (Jer. 42:10). It hurt the Lord to hurt His people: "In all their distress He too was distressed" (Is. 63:9); "And He could bear Israel's misery no longer" (Judg. 10:16). He can hardly bear it today.

How did God feel during the Crusades, the Inquisitions and the Holocaust? There is no doubt that He "suffered" with His people. Shouldn't we suffer with Him? Even when Israel was being judged for its sins, the Lord denounced the mistreatment it endured:

> Thus said the Lord of Hosts: I am very jealous for Jerusalem—for Zion—and I am very angry with those nations that are at ease; for I was only angry a little, but they overdid the punishment (Zech. 1:14-15, New Jewish Version).

They took the judgment too far, so judgment overtook them.

Paul was a man who certainly knew the heart of God, and he drank deeply from the wells of God's joy. Yet while "always rejoicing," Paul was "sorrowful" too (2 Cor. 6:10). This was his personal testimony:

> I speak the truth in Christ—I am not lying, my conscience confirms it in the Holy Spirit—I have *great sorrow* and *unceasing anguish* in my heart. For I could wish that I myself were cursed and cut off from Christ for the sake of my brothers, those of my own race, the people of Israel... (Rom. 9:1-4).

True love afflicts the heart. Only true love will do.[5]

Jesus wept when He saw the dark future of His people. He had come to bring them light! But for almost 2000 years now, each day has had its share of pain. Concentration camp survivor and Nazi hunter Simon Wiesenthal has compiled a chronicle of Jewish martyrdom for every day of the year. Here is merely *one typical day*, selected at random from Wiesenthal's chronicle, in the agonizing history of our people.[6] All these tragedies occurred on June 23, one day out of many in our people's saga of sorrow:

1270 In Weissenbur, Germany, 7 Jews are arrested without charges held against them, tortured, and executed.

1298 The Rindfleish Persecutions...annihilated 146 Jewish communities in southern and central Germany. In Windsheim in Franconia 55 Jews are burned at the stake; 900 Jews of the large community of Wurzburg are slain, among them 100 who had sought refuge there from other places. In the little town of Neustadt on the Aisch River, 71 Jews are burned to death.

1475 In the case of Simon of Trent (Italy), a Christian child is found dead and Samuel, a wealthy Jew, and others of his brethren are falsely accused and subjected to torture. The boy is proclaimed a martyr and the Jews are kept imprisoned and tortured from March to April. On June 23, Samuel is burned at the stake and the others burned or broken on the wheel. Simon of Trent is venerated as a martyr until the intervention of the Vatican in 1965.

1919 During a pogrom, 45 Jews are slaughtered, many are severely wounded, and 35 Jewish women are raped by [army] insurgents...in Skvira, Kiev.

1941 After the Germans invade Sokal, Poland (today Ukrainian S.S.R.), where 6,000 Jews live, 8 Jews are shot....

1942 The SS murders 850 Jews in Wielopole, in the district of Cracow, Poland.

The first selection for the gas chambers in the Auschwitz extermination camp in Poland takes place on the platform of the train arriving from Paris, France....

1943 A deportation train leaves Paris for Auschwitz, carrying 1,000 Jews, among them 100 children under the age of 16 and 13 babies, who are all killed upon arrival.

All inmates of the Jewish home for the aged of Moravska Ostrava, Czechoslovakia, are deported to Auschwitz....

A deportation train with 1,018 Jewish people leaves from the Drancy transit camp in the German occupied zone of France for Auschwitz. On their arrival, 518 are gassed; 72 men and 37 women will survive.

Jewish history is still being written.
Only more tears can change the script.

Chapter Eleven

So Near and Yet So Far

> The Psalmist said, "I have set the Lord before me, always" (Psa. 16:8). This is a cardinal principle of the Torah and a fundamental principle of life among the pious who walk before the Lord. For the attitude, dealings and conversation of a man when in the presence of a king are not the same as when he is in his own home, among family and friends. How much more will a man be careful with his words and deeds if he but realise that the King of Kings, "whose Glory fills the whole earth" (Isa. 6:3), watches over him and observes his deeds, as it is written: "If a man should hide himself in secret places, will I not see him? saith the Lord" (Jer. 23:24). Bearing this in mind, a man will acquire reverence for God, humility and piety, and will be ashamed to do anything wrong (Rabbi Moses Isserles).[1]

These beautiful words form the opening comments to the standard Jewish code of Law. For the religious Jew, the Law is a deeply *spiritual* thing because the Jew's life is supposed to be lived entirely before the Lord. Every detail is important. Every action counts. *Everything* must be made holy—the way he eats, the way he talks, the way he deals in business, even the way he conducts himself in the bathroom!

> Bar Kappara [a sage of the Talmud] expounded: What short
> text is there upon which all the essential principles of the
> Torah depend? *In all thy ways acknowledge Him and He will
> direct thy paths* (Prov. 3:6).[2]

In the words of contemporary author Rabbi Zechariah
Fendel, the Jew must remember:

> that Torah consists, not only of ritual laws and testimonial
> statutes, not only of laws concerning prayers and bene-
> dictions, Sabbath and festivals, but that it is, rather, an all-
> encompassing law, which serves to guide the Torah Jew in
> virtually all his endeavors....When the individual leaves the
> Synagogue each morning and prepares to enter the world of
> business, he should not regard this as though he had stepped
> out of a spiritual world into a world of crass materialism,
> which is entirely devoid of spiritual values. On the contrary,
> he should carry the spiritual values of the Synagogue and
> *Bais HaMidrash* [House of Study] with him into his busi-
> ness world.[3]

Even the secular must be sanctified.

When he rises in the morning, the religious Jew says
these words in Hebrew:

> I gratefully thank You, O living and eternal King, for You
> have returned my soul within me with compassion—abun-
> dant is Your faithfulness![4]

As he washes his hands, always following the same
routine, he says:

> The beginning of wisdom is the fear of the Lord—good un-
> derstanding to all their practitioners; His praise endures
> forever [Ps. 111:10]. Blessed is the Name of His glorious
> kingdom for all eternity.[5]

He recites a short blessing before eating his meals, and a lengthy blessing *after* eating his meals. (The after-meal prayers are about five pages long!) Some Jews, before beginning their bedtime prayers, say:

> Master of the Universe, behold, I forgive every one who has injured me: and may no one be punished because of his wrong to me![6]

This is how the Orthodox Jew seeks to live his life before God. He sees himself as a child of the Lord's special covenant with Israel. He must be separated and he must be devoted. His beliefs are reflected in his prayers—and reinforced whenever he prays. The *Siddur*, the Jewish prayer book, filled with hundreds of Scripture verses and dozens of rabbinic compositions, is greatly beloved.

Eliezer Berkovits relates:

> Zalman Kleinman, one of the witnesses at the Eichmann trial, told how one day, as he was lying in his bunk in the children's barracks at Auschwitz, he noticed the second-in-command in the barracks walking towards someone in order to punish him with a rubber truncheon. Since the truncheon was a more recent replacement for the traditional stick, which often broke in the middle of the beating, he got up from his bunk to see how this new instrument worked, so that he could know what to expect should he himself one day have to encounter it. The boy who was to be punished was ordered to come down from his bunk and to bend over. Surrounded by a group of children, he was beaten. The boy neither cried, nor even so much as moaned or sighed. The customary twenty-five lashes was increased to thirty, forty. But the boy was still completely silent. When the number fifty had been reached, the German fell into a fit of madness and started beating the boy all over his body. Yet not a sound

was heard from the lad—he was fourteen years old and did not cry. When the officer left, the victim was lifted from the floor by the other boys. Having recovered somewhat from the beating, he responded to their inquiry as to the reason for the punishment by saying, "It was well worthwhile. I brought several prayerbooks to my friends."[7]

One of the favorite prayers of the rabbis is called *Adon Olam*, "Lord of the World" (or, "Master of the Universe").[8] It was written almost 1000 years ago by the great Spanish Jewish poet Solomon Ibn Gabirol. Every morning and at night, immediately before sleep, these words are sung in prayer:

> Lord of the world, He reigned alone
> While yet the universe was naught,
> When by His will all things were wrought,
> Then first His sov'ran name was known.

> And when the All shall cease to be,
> In dread lone splendour He shall reign,
> He was, He is, He shall remain
> In glorious eternity.

> For He is one, no second shares
> His nature or His loneliness;
> Unending and beginningless,
> All strength is His, all sway He bears.

> He is the living God to save,
> My Rock while sorrow's toils endure,
> My banner and My stronghold sure,
> The cup of life whene'er I crave.

I place my soul within His palm
Before I sleep as when I wake,
And though my body I forsake,
Rest in the Lord in fearless calm.[9]

Now, read the last two stanzas again and consider this: These words are often sung "*by those who watch the last moments of one who is departing this life*" (Rabbi J. H. Hertz, my italics). Does this touch the depths of your heart?

In Judaism, the dead are not quickly forgotten. There is a prayer in their memory called the *Kaddish,* offered up daily for eleven months after the loved one's departure and then once each year on the anniversary of their death. It is not a prayer *for* the dead, but a hymn of thanksgiving to God with supplication for His redemption. This is what the Jewish people are taught to pray:

> May His great Name grow exalted and sanctified in the world that He created as He willed. May He give reign to His kingship in your lifetimes and in your days, and in the lifetimes of the entire Family of Israel, swiftly and soon. Now respond: Amen. May His great Name be blessed forever and ever.

> Blessed, praised, glorified, exalted, extolled, mighty, upraised, and lauded be the Name of the Holy One. Blessed is He beyond any blessing and song, praise and consolation that are uttered in the world. Now respond: Amen. May there be abundant peace from Heaven, and life, upon us and upon all Israel. Now respond: Amen.[10]

All the prayers we have just read, and many other prayers of confession and repentance, praise and adoration, request and supplication, have been prayed by religious

Jews worldwide today. Yet these people do not know Jesus at all, even though He is the very revelation of the Father. In spite of their fervor and commitment, they still fall short of the mark. They earnestly seek to approach the Lord, yet they are still serving Him from a distance. Can we join our prayers together with theirs, that God would make Himself known to them?

Jews, much like Job in the Bible, are often brutally honest with God. They literally "have it out" with Him. If only He would speak to them from heaven, just like He spoke to Job!

Zvi Kolitz, in the name and spirit of Yossel Rakover, wrote this prayer against the flaming backdrop of the Holocaust. Here are just a few of the lines. They are crying for a divine response!

> ...I believe in You, God of Israel, even though You have done everything to stop me from believing in You. I believe in Your laws even if I cannot excuse Your actions....

> I want to say to You that now, more than in any previous period of our eternal path of agony, we, we the tortured, the humiliated, the buried alive, the burned alive, we the insulted, the mocked, the lonely, the forsaken by God and man—we have the right to know *what are the limits of Your forbearance?*

> I should like to say something more: Do not put the rope under too much strain, lest, alas, it snap! The test to which You have put us is so severe, so unbearably severe, that You should—You must—forgive those members of Your people who, in their misery, have turned from You....

> You have done everything to make me stop believing in You. Now lest it seem to You that You will succeed by these

tribulations to drive me from the right path, I notify You, my God and God of my father, *that it will not avail You in the least!* You may insult me, You may castigate me, You may take from me all that I cherish and hold dear in the world, You may torture me to death—I shall believe in *You*, I shall love You no matter what You do to test me!

And these are my last words to You, my wrathful God: nothing will avail You in the least. You have done everything to make me renounce You, to make me lose faith in You, but I die exactly as I have lived, a believer!

Eternally praised be the God of the dead, the God of vengeance, of truth and of law, Who will soon show His face to the world again and shake its foundations with His almighty voice.

Hear, O Israel, the Lord our God, the Lord is One.
Into Your hands, O Lord, I consign my soul.[11]

No one "wrestles with God" like the Jew. Can we also wrestle with Him—for them? Rend your heart, bare your soul and feel the pain of the Jews.

Every day observant Jews everywhere recite these words:

I believe with complete faith in the coming of the Messiah, and even though he delay, I will wait for him every day that he will come.[12]

Can we ask the Lord, the Master of the Universe and our Father, to reveal to them that Messiah *has* come?

As they pray three times daily,[13]

Bring us back, our Father, to Your Torah, and bring us near, our King, to Your service, and influence us to return in perfect repentance before You. Blessed are You, O Lord, Who desires repentance—

let us lift *our* voices in intercession and say, "Grant them a true spirit of repentance, Lord, through the power of Messiah's blood!"

As they cry out three times daily,

Forgive us, our Father, for we have erred; pardon us, our King, for we have willfully sinned; for You pardon and forgive. Blessed are You, O Lord, the gracious One Who pardons abundantly—

let us lift *our* voices in intercession and say, "Forgive and pardon them fully, Lord, through the power of Messiah's blood!"

As they make their requests known before God three times daily, saying,

Behold our affliction, take up our grievance, and redeem us speedily for Your Name's sake, for You are a powerful Redeemer. Blessed are You, O Lord, Redeemer of Israel—

let us lift *our* voices in intercession and say, "Redeem and deliver them quickly, Lord, through the power of Messiah's blood!"

As they lift up their petitions three times daily, saying,

Heal us, O Lord—then we will be healed; save us—then we will be saved, for You are our praise. Bring complete recovery for all our ailments, for You are God, King, the faithful and compassionate Healer. Blessed are You, O Lord, Who heals the sick of His people Israel—

let us lift *our* voices in intercession and say, "Heal the wounds of Your suffering people, Lord, restore them and make them whole, through the power of Messiah's blood!"

And as they ask God to accept their requests three times daily, praying:

> Hear our voice, O Lord our God, pity and be compassionate to us, and accept—with compassion and favor—our prayer, for God Who hears prayers and supplications are You. From before Yourself, our King, turn us not away empty-handed, for You hear the prayer of Your people with compassion. Blessed are You, O Lord, Who hears prayer—

let us fall on our faces, lift up our voices, cry out from our hearts, plead with the Lord and say, "Father, hear! Father, act! Father, look down and see—and be merciful, Lord, to Your covenant people. Do not turn them away!"

No people is so near and yet so far.

Chapter Twelve

Has God Forsaken His People?

Some things are non-negotiable. God's covenant with Israel is one of them. How could He have made Himself more clear?

He gave His oath to Abram, and reiterated it *six more times* to Abraham, to his son Isaac and to his grandson Jacob. On one occasion,

> When God made His promise to Abraham, since there was no one greater for Him to swear by, He swore by Himself (Heb. 6:13).

Why did God speak so decisively? It was because He

> wanted to make the unchanging nature of His purpose very clear to the heirs of what was promised, [so] He confirmed it with an oath (Heb. 6:17).

God Who cannot lie bound Himself by an oath!

His covenant with Israel was reiterated through Moses, repeated by the prophets and rehearsed by the psalmists.

Jesus Himself affirmed it (Matt. 19:28), Paul articulated it (Rom. 9-11) and the gates of the New Jerusalem announce it forever (Rev. 22:11-12). God has chosen Israel as His covenant people.

What if Israel broke the covenant? What would then happen to them? Listen to these unmistakably clear truths:

> …Though I completely destroy all the nations among which I scatter you, I will not completely destroy you. I will discipline you but only with justice; I will not let you go entirely unpunished (Jer. 30:11).

The exact same words are repeated in Jeremiah 46:28. God will completely destroy other nations, but He will not completely destroy Israel! He treats His people differently from other people; they are judged more strictly, but they will never be wiped out.

No matter what Israel does, God will never forsake them as a distinct people. In Jeremiah 31:31-34, the Lord declares that He will make a new covenant with Israel and Judah. But He doesn't stop there. It's as if He's saying, "Now, don't get Me wrong! Don't think that this new covenant means that I'm abandoning My people. No!"[1]

> This is what the LORD says, He who appoints the sun to shine by day, who decrees the moon and stars to shine by night, who stirs up the sea so that its waves roar—the LORD Almighty is His name: "Only if these decrees vanish from My sight," declares the LORD, "will the descendants of Israel ever cease to be a nation before Me." This is what the LORD says: "Only if the heavens above can be measured and the foundations of the earth below be searched out will I reject

all the descendants of Israel because of all they have done," declares the LORD (Jer. 31:35-37).

As long as there is a sun, moon, stars, earth and sea, there will be a distinct people of Israel—no matter what they do. It's God's promise! It's true![2]

"Is not Ephraim my dear son, the child in whom I delight? Though I often speak against him, I shall remember him. Therefore My heart yearns for him, I have great compassion for him," declares the Lord (Jer. 31:20).[3]

Look at how relevant God's prophetic word is to our day and age. For centuries the Church, in arrogance, because of ignorance, claimed that she alone was the true Israel, that she had replaced the ancient covenant people. The Church taught that it was the Christians alone who were the true Jews. (How strange that these Christians were not claiming to be Jewish during the Holocaust!) The Church taught emphatically that the physical people of Israel (those who were ethnically Jewish and those who joined the nation through conversion to Judaism) were eternally rejected.[4]

This is not some worn-out old doctrine. It is on the increase again in our day.[5] Yet the Lord is not surprised. Twenty-five hundred years ago, He already addressed this issue:

The word of the LORD came to Jeremiah: "Have you not noticed that these people are saying, 'The LORD has rejected the two kingdoms He chose?' So they despise My people and no longer regard them as a nation. This is what the LORD says: 'If I have not established My covenant with day and night and the fixed laws of heaven and earth, then I will reject the descendants of Jacob and David My servant and will not choose one of his sons to rule over the descendants of Abraham, Isaac and Jacob. For I will restore their fortunes and have compassion on them' " (Jer. 33:23-26).

People are still murmuring against Israel and despising the people and the nation. God's answer is still the same: "I will never reject them!"

What exactly did God promise Abraham and his descendants? How long are His promises good? Psalm 105 has the answer for us.

> He remembers His covenant *forever,* the word He commanded for *a thousand generations,* the covenant He made with Abraham, the oath He swore to Isaac. He confirmed it to Jacob as a decree, to Israel as an *everlasting* covenant: "To you I will give the land of Canaan as the portion you will inherit" (Ps. 105:8-11).

Did God make Himself clear?

The Scriptures speak of God's *covenant,* the *word* He *commanded,* His *oath* which He *confirmed* as a *decree* forever, for a thousand generations, as an everlasting covenant. The Lord is trying to make a point!

Not only did He promise to bless Abraham and make him into a great nation; not only did He promise to multiply his seed; not only did He promise to make him the father of many nations; not only did He promise to bless those who blessed him and curse those who cursed him; He also promised Abraham the land of Canaan, with clearly defined borders, as an everlasting inheritance to his natural descendants—until this earth is no more.

Amazingly, some teachers have tried to get out of this perpetual land promise to Israel. They claim that in the New Testament, neither Jesus nor the apostles ever reiterate this particular aspect of the covenant.[6] But why should they reiterate it? When almost all of the New Testament was being written, about one million Jews were living in the Land, Jerusalem was the spiritual and national capitol and the Temple was still standing. And Jesus made it clear that, despite Jerusalem's soon-coming destruction—a destruction that would last "until the times of the Gentiles are fulfilled"—He would *come back* to a Jewish Jerusalem (Luke 21:24; Matt. 23:37-39).[7] Obviously Jews would be in the Land!

But there is another reason why Jesus and the apostles did not *explicitly* stress the land promise to their people. The specifics of God's covenant with the patriarchs were so clearly stated in the Scriptures that it would have been a waste of words to repeat them all! David Brown, the respected nineteenth century Bible commentator, was correct when he said:

> *What is permanent in the kingdom of God under the Old Testament is* PRESUMED *in the New.*[8]

And let all believers who question Israel's right to the Land, *based on the New Testament,* take note of this: The New Testament doesn't state that Israel would be exiled *from* the Land either! *Both* of these Old Testament truths, Israel's scattering and Israel's regathering, are presumed in the New.[9]

The covenant God made with Israel is just like the covenant He made with David. The Lord declared to David that He would establish a lasting dynasty for him:

> When your days are over and you rest with your fathers, I will raise up your offspring to succeed you, who will come from your own body, and I will establish his kingdom....I will be his father, and he will be My son. When he does wrong, I will punish him with the rod of men, with floggings inflicted by men. But My love will never be taken away from him, as I took it away from Saul, whom I removed from before you. Your house and your kingdom will endure forever before Me; your throne will be established forever (2 Sam. 7:12-16).

What a wonderful word! In spite of David's terrible sin and Solomon's tragic backsliding, in spite of the godlessness of Davidic kings like Ahaz and Manasseh, the kingdom would never be taken from his physical descendants.

When the kingdom was divided and God gave Jeroboam the ten northern tribes, He did so to humble David's descendants, "but not forever" (1 Kin. 11:39). He still left one tribe with the sons of David,

> so that David My servant may always have a lamp before Me in Jerusalem, the city where I chose to put My Name (1 Kin. 11:36).

God offered a lasting dynasty to Jeroboam and his off-spring *on the condition* that he keep the Lord's statutes as David had done (1 Kin. 11:38). But when Jeroboam failed to obey, his dynasty was wiped out completely, while the kingdom of David lived on. And it continues to live on today: The King of kings and Lord of lords is a direct descendant of David! God was faithful to keep His word.

He is just as faithful to keep His word to Israel. *His covenant with Abraham is just as unconditional and everlasting as His covenant with David.* Read Genesis 15 carefully. In ancient days, that is how covenants were made.

Sacrificial animals were cut in two and their severed bodies placed in two lines. *Both parties* entering into the covenant would then walk between the carcasses. By doing so they were symbolically saying, "If I break this binding agreement, if I fail to uphold my side of the pact, then let me suffer the same fate that these animals have suffered." But something was different in Genesis 15. Only God passed through the pieces! This was a one-way deal.[10]

When the sun had set and darkness had fallen, a smoking firepot with a blazing torch appeared and passed between the pieces. On that day the LORD made a covenant with Abram and said, "To your descendants I give this land, from the river of Egypt to the great river, the Euphrates—the land of the Kenites, Kenizzites, Kadmonites, Hittites, Perizzites, Rephaites, Amorites, Canaanites, Girgashites and Jebusites" (Gen. 15:17-21).

The Land belonged to other nations. But at the proper time it would be given to Abraham's seed.

If they violated the terms of the covenant—especially as expressed through Moses—then they would be punished and even driven temporarily from the Land. But just as God's word to David stands firm, His word to Abraham endures, *no matter what Israel does.* This is what He said through Moses. When the Israelites are

...in the land of their enemies, I will not reject them or abhor them so as to destroy them completely, breaking My covenant with them. I am the LORD their God. But for their sake I will remember the covenant with their ancestors whom I brought out of Egypt in the sight of the nations to be their God. I am the LORD (Lev. 26:44-45).

The LORD will scatter you among the peoples, and only a few of you will survive among the nations to which the LORD will drive you....When you are in distress and all these things have happened to you, then in later days you will return to the LORD your God and obey Him. For the LORD your God is a merciful God; He will not abandon or destroy you or forget the covenant with your forefathers, which He confirmed to them by oath (Deut. 4:27, 30-31).

Even today, when

As far as the gospel is concerned, they are enemies on [our] account; [yet] as far as election is concerned, they are loved *on account of the patriarchs,* for God's gifts and His call are irrevocable (Rom. 11:28-29).[11]

Could anything be more plain?

Right now the great majority of the Jewish people are our "enemies," "as far as the gospel is concerned." They reject our message (the Orthodox Jews reject it most strongly), and some even actively oppose it.[12] As individuals, they forfeit their covenant blessings when they turn from Jesus the Messiah. But as a people, they are still elect and loved "on account of the patriarchs." Otherwise, God's promises have no meaning and election has no significance. "Abraham, I'm swearing by Myself, I'm putting My reputation on the line. I will bless your offspring always—no matter what. (But I may replace them with someone else one day!)" That is not the Lord that we serve.

God's covenant with Abraham is just as unconditional and everlasting as His covenant with the Church. The Lord "saved us, not because of righteous things we had done, but because of His mercy" (Titus 3:5). Praise God, we were chosen by grace! But we are not the only recipients of the Lord's unmerited favor. To Israel, Moses said:

> The LORD did not set His affection on you and choose you because you were more numerous than other peoples, for you were the fewest of all peoples. But it was because the LORD loved you and kept the oath He swore to your forefathers that He brought you out with a mighty hand and redeemed you from the land of slavery, from the power of Pharaoh king of Egypt (Deut. 7:7-8).

Sounds familiar, doesn't it? God's covenants with Israel and with the Church are based on His promise, not our performance.

Old Testament Israel and the New Testament Church both stood, and still stand, by grace.[13] Both received God's eternal promises. Together we make up the family of God: The faithful ones of Israel and the chosen ones from every nation become one new man out of the two, one body, one people.

> For through Him [Jesus!] we both have access to the Father by one Spirit (Eph. 2:18).

Great is the wisdom of God.

This is not what the Muslims believe. It is a fundamental tenet of the Koran that both Israel and the Church failed. Moses was a prophet. Jesus was a prophet. But Muhammad was the seal of the prophets, the messenger of the final revelation. The Jews are not the people of God—they failed! The Christians are not the people of God—they failed! It is the Muslims who are the people of God.[14]

Of course, this is preposterous. But, in the event that you are still uncertain about the calling of Israel, consider this simple truth: If God could *forsake* Israel, in spite of His unconditional, everlasting promises, then He could forsake the Church! If God could *replace* Israel, in spite of His unconditional, everlasting promises, then He could replace the Church! So, if you hold to a theology that says, "God has forsaken physical Israel," or "The Church has replaced Israel," you had better be extremely careful.

Maybe the Koran is right!

Chapter Thirteen

Natural Children and God's Children

Romans is Paul's theological masterpiece. In the first eleven chapters, he lays out the absolute essentials of our faith. In the last five chapters, he tells us how to live. If we understand Romans, we understand the gospel.

It is in Romans that Paul demonstrates that all have sinned, Jew and Gentile alike. It is here that he opens up the incredible revelation of justification by faith. (Think of trying to understand that without Romans!) It is here that he speaks of our struggle with sin, our victory over sin and life in the Spirit of God. And then he brings it all to a climax with an in-depth teaching about *Israel*.[1]

Beginning in Romans 9, Paul speaks of the special role of the people of Israel, his brothers, those of his own race:

...Theirs is the adoption as sons; theirs the divine glory, the covenants, the receiving of the law, the temple worship and the promises. Theirs are the patriarchs, and from them is traced the human ancestry of Christ, who is God over all, forever praised! Amen (Rom. 9:4-5).

What an awesome calling!

But there is a question: Did God's word fail? If the people of Israel were the special recipients of God's promises, why have most of them rejected the Messiah? Why are they living outside the *New* Covenant if they are the covenant people? Paul has a simple answer:

> It is not as though God's word had failed. For not all who are descended from Israel are Israel. Nor because they are his descendants are they all Abraham's children....In other words, it is not the natural children who are God's children, but it is the children of the promise who are regarded as Abraham's offspring (Rom. 9:6-8).

Now that should have settled the question. There are *natural children* and there are *God's children.* "Natural children" refers to the people of Israel as a whole; "God's children" refers to the believing remnant within Israel. So there is Israel (the natural children) and there is Israel (the spiritual children). There is an Israel *within* Israel.[2] It really isn't that complicated!

We can draw a similar parallel with the "Church." (Please bear in mind that this is only a rough parallel.) There are natural children (those born into a Christian family) and there are God's children (those born from above into His heavenly family). There is the Church (all who call themselves Christians) and there is the Church (those whom God calls Christians). To rephrase and reapply Paul: "Not all who are in the Church are the Church. There is the Church *within* the Church."

But—this is of vital importance—pious Buddhists or Muslims are not the true Church. Of course not! The true Church consists of believers *within* the Church, not religious people *outside* the Church. It is only those within the Church (i.e., those who profess the Christian faith) who can possibly be the true Church. In the same way, Paul never said that Gentile believers were "true" or "spiritual" Israel. It was the believing remnant *within* Israel that was "true" or "spiritual" Israel. (Actually, the terms "true Israel" or "spiritual Israel" never occur in the Bible, and it might be helpful to completely avoid them.)

Many people have feelings and impressions about what the Scriptures teach. But the facts are facts: While the New Testament often describes Israel and the Church in similar terms—both are pictured as the children of God, the bride of God, the chosen people, etc.—*on no definite occasion does the New Testament ever call the Church, "Israel."*[3] In fact, out of the 77 times that the words "Israel" and "Israelite" occur in the Greek New Testament, there are only *two* verses in which "Israel" could *possibly* refer to the Church as a whole: Galatians 6:16, where Paul speaks of the "Israel of God" and Revelation 7:4, where John speaks of the 144,000 sealed from the twelve tribes of Israel. This is saying something! Seventy-five "definites" and only two "maybes." I wouldn't want to side with the "maybes"!

As for the verses open to dispute, in Galatians 6:16 the King James Version, the New King James Version and the New American Standard Bible all imply the same thing: "The Israel of God" does not refer to the whole Church. It refers to believing Jews.[4] The same can be said for the description of the 144,000 sealed in Revelation 7:4. It most probably describes the final harvest of Jews worldwide. Elsewhere in the Book of Revelation "Israel" means "Israel" (Rev. 2:14) and "the twelve tribes of Israel" mean "the twelve tribes of Israel," as distinguished from "the twelve apostles" (Rev. 21:12-14).[5]

Even if someone insisted on understanding Galatians 6:16 and Revelation 7:4 differently,[6] everyone who knows anything about interpreting the Word knows this: We never build a doctrine on just one or two verses, especially if the meaning of the verses is disputed! And who would ever dream of erecting a theological system on the foundation of *one verse in the midst of a symbolic vision in Revelation?* I lovingly challenge all those who claim that the entire Church is "Israel" to find two verses *anywhere* in the Bible that *indisputably* state this "fact." They simply are not there! When God said "Israel," He meant the natural children, either in whole or in part.

What about Romans 2:28-29? Didn't Paul say there that Gentiles who believed were true Jews? Look carefully at these verses as translated in the New International Version (I have added the italics):

> A man is not a Jew if he is *only* one outwardly, nor is circumcision *merely* outward and physical. No, a man is a Jew if he is one inwardly; and circumcision is circumcision of the heart, by the Spirit, not by the written code. Such a man's praise is not from men, but from God.

In other words, *between two Jews,* one who is only circumcised physically, and the other who is also circumcised spiritually, which one is the real Jew, the Jew in this special sense? The answer is obvious: The one who is also circumcised spiritually!

But is Paul saying here that believing Gentiles are also Jews in this special sense? Most probably not. He is directing his argument to Jews, primarily to unsaved Jews, in Romans 2:17-29. *Within that context* he is defining who is the real Jew—spiritually speaking. And in the rest of the Greek New Testament, the word "Jew" occurs over 190 times, referring clearly to ethnic, national Jews. More than 190 "definites" and only a couple of "maybes"![7] Are there any takers for the "maybe" position?

Even if someone understood Romans 2:28-29 to say that believing Gentiles were spiritual Jews (it is easy from the text to see why many Christians believe this about themselves[8]) that would not change this important fact: Paul never said that natural Jews were no longer Jews. He only said that natural Jews were not Jews in this *special, fuller* sense.[9] Just keep reading his letter! After making his point in Romans 2:28-29 (remember, it is one of the few times in the entire New Testament that the word Jew is used like this), he goes back to referring to *all* Jews in the normal way.

If you have any doubt, read the *very next verse.*

What advantage, then, is there in being a *Jew,* or what value is there in circumcision? Much in every way!...(Rom. 3:1- 2).

In other words, since being a Jew outwardly and physically doesn't guarantee a right relationship with God, what's the advantage in being a Jew, *a physically circumcised, ethnic Jew?* Much in every way, because God entrusted His Word to His physical, natural people—the Jews! It really is quite simple.

If Paul was teaching that natural Jews were no longer Jews and that believing Gentiles were the real Jews, what in the world did he mean in Romans 3:9?

> ...We have already made the charge that Jews and Gentiles alike are all under sin.

If Jews are not Jews and Gentiles are not Gentiles, what was Paul trying to say in Romans 3:29?

> Is God the God of Jews only? Is He not the God of Gentiles too? Yes, of Gentiles too.

And what then would be the meaning of Romans 15:27, if believing Gentiles are now Jews?

> ...For if the Gentiles have shared in the Jews' spiritual blessings, they owe it to the Jews to share with them their material blessings.

Clearly, Gentile means Gentile and Jew means Jew!

It is one thing to argue that *once* or *twice* Paul used the words "Israel" and "Jew" *in a special sense,* referring to the whole Church as "the Israel of God" and all believers as "Jews." (Although I personally disagree with this, I certainly wouldn't call this position dangerous.) But it is another thing entirely to turn around and ignore the remaining 268 New Testament references to "Israel" and "Jew" and claim that Israel is no longer Israel and Jews are no longer Jews! *That* most certainly is dangerous.

It is one thing to say, "Paul used the word 'circumcision' in a special sense (Phil. 3:3) to refer to all believers." It is another thing to say, "Those who are physically circumcised on the eighth day are no longer counted as Jews!" Even the Book of Deuteronomy recognized two circumcisions: circumcision of the flesh and circumcision of the heart. But one did not negate the other! In the words of the internationally acclaimed Romans commentator, C. E. B. Cranfield, Paul's statement in Romans 2:28-29 "should not be taken as implying that those who are Jews only outwardly are excluded from the promises."[10] Absolutely not!

All of God's covenants were made with Israel *as a whole*. No one can deny that. At Mount Sinai, He spoke to the entire nation! But only God's children, *the faithful within Israel*, enjoyed the covenant blessings. And what does God say to the rest of the people? Does He say, "You are no longer My natural children"? No! Instead He says, "Turn back, O backturning children; I will heal your backslidings" (Jer. 3:22, my translation).[11] The covenant promise still stands.

As basic as this is, later Church interpreters went beyond the meaning of the Word. First they said, "You see, it is not all who are descended from Israel who are Israel. It is the true believers who are Israel, and we are the true believers! We are Israel! It's not just believing *Jews* who are Israel. *Everyone* who believes is part of Israel too!"[12]

What's so terrible about saying this? Maybe nothing so far. But the next step was simply disastrous: If the Church is spiritual Israel, the new Israel, then there is no need for *natural* Israel, the *old* Israel anymore. "Let them rot for all we care! They've lost the blessing forever. They crucified the Messiah. They blew their opportunity. In fact, they still don't believe their own Scriptures. They are no longer the covenant people. We are!"[13]

To a great degree, the horrors described in the previous chapters of this book are a by-product of this very theology.

It would not have been a problem if Gentile Christians had simply said: "God has *expanded* the borders of Israel! Now we are included among the covenant people since we are the spiritual seed of Abraham. And we look forward to the day when the Lord will restore the physical seed of Abraham too! The Old Testament 'Church' consisted of Israel alone, but the New Testament 'Church' consists of Israel and us. Together we are the new Israel!" Many devout Christians have held to this belief—and there is much truth to it—without for a moment thinking that God's promises to the natural children were ever in doubt.[14]

But for many Christians, the notion that the Church was the new Israel meant that God had forever discarded His children after the flesh. "Away with the old! The new has come! You Jews are eternally cursed!" Reinhold Mayer, the German New Testament scholar, put it very simply:

> The path of Gentile Christianity turned from Judaism and led into Gentile anti-Semitism, which was on the increase after the [destruction of Jerusalem in 70 C.E.]. The prophets' criticism of Israel was misunderstood as anti-Jewish and repeated irresponsibly. Even when the words were kept their meaning was distorted to imply the opposite, and this served to sharpen Gentile hatred of Jews.[15]

Paul knew how important it was for the Gentile believers to understand the place of Israel. That's why he devoted so much space—three whole chapters of his most in-depth epistle—to the subject of Israel's divine call. Many believers say, "Yes, it's true. Paul talked a lot about Israel in Romans 9-11, but he was talking about *spiritual* Israel. Remember what he said: 'not all who are descended from Israel are Israel' (Rom. 9:6). When Paul said that 'all Israel will be saved' (Rom. 11:26) he really didn't mean *all* Israel."

Well, why don't we let Paul speak for himself? Let's allow Paul to interpret Paul. When he said "Israel" in Romans 9-11, did he mean the natural children or God's children?

> **Romans 9:1-5**—Paul had "great sorrow and unceasing anguish" in his heart for *Israel.* Which "Israel" did he mean? The natural children! But someone may object, "That was *before* he said that 'not all who are descended from Israel are Israel.' What about after that verse? Didn't he change the meaning of Israel?" Let's read *all* the remaining references to "Israel" (and "Israelite") in Romans 9-11. The truth will set us free!

> **Romans 9:27**—"Isaiah cries out concerning *Israel:* 'Though the number of *Israelites* be like the sand of the sea, only the remnant will be saved.'" Which "Israel/Israelites" did Paul mean? The natural children!

> **Romans 9:31**—"But *Israel,* who pursued a law of righteousness, has not attained it." Which "Israel" did Paul mean? The natural children!

Romans 10:1—"Brothers, my heart's desire and prayer to God for the *Israelites*[16] is that they may be saved." Which "Israelites" did Paul mean? The natural children!

Romans 10:16—"But not all the *Israelites* accepted the good news...." Which "Israelites" did Paul mean? The natural children!

Romans 10:19-21—"Again I ask: Did *Israel* not understand?...concerning *Israel* He says, 'All day long I have held out my hands to a disobedient and obstinate people." Which "Israel" did Paul mean? The natural children!

Romans 11:1-2—"I ask then: Did God reject His people? By no means! I am an *Israelite* myself, a descendant of Abraham, from the tribe of Benjamin. God did not reject His people, whom He foreknew...." Which "Israelites" did Paul mean? The natural children! The literal descendants! Paul was *one of them*. That was his whole point. He continues this thought in the rest of the verse.

Romans 11:2—"...Don't you know what the Scripture says in the passage about Elijah—how he appealed to God against *Israel*." Which "Israel" did Paul mean? The natural children! It was *among them* that God had preserved a remnant (Rom. 11:3-5).

Romans 11:7—"What then? What *Israel* sought so earnestly it did not obtain, but the elect did.

The others were hardened." Which "Israel" did Paul mean? The natural children! Only the elect, God's children, those whom He foreknew, obtained righteousness; the others, the rest of the natural children, were hardened.

Romans 11:11—"Again I ask: Did they [the natural children] stumble so as to fall beyond recovery? Not at all! [Let the Church repeat these words out loud: Israel did not stumble beyond recovery.] Rather, because of their transgression [the transgression of the natural children], salvation has come to the Gentiles to make *Israel* envious." Which "Israel" did Paul mean? The natural children! And look at verse 13: "I am talking to you Gentiles...." Paul is talking *to* the Gentile believers *about* Israel. He is not telling the Gentile believers that they *are* Israel! And now we get to the heart of it all...

Romans 11:25—"I do not want you to be ignorant of this mystery, brothers, so that you may not be conceited: *Israel* has experienced a hardening in part until the full number of Gentiles has come in." Which "Israel" did Paul mean? The natural children! They were the ones who were hardened. And what will happen to this very same Israel when the "full number of the Gentiles has come in"?

Romans 11:26-27—"And so all *Israel* will be saved...." Which "Israel" did Paul mean? The *natural children! Glory and praise to God! "And so ALL ISRAEL WILL BE SAVED, as it is written: 'The Deliverer will come from Zion; He will turn godlessness away from Jacob. And this is My covenant with them* [Israel, the natural children] *when I take away their sins.'"*

The "Israel" that was hardened in part is the "Israel" that will be saved! The "Israel" that did not obtain righteousness is the "Israel" that will obtain it! "Because of *their* transgression, salvation has come to the Gentiles," because of "*their* disobedience" the Gentiles "have now received mercy" (Rom. 11:11, 30). Now, because of God's mercy to the Gentiles "*they* too may now receive mercy" (Rom. 11:31). And mercy they will receive!

Yes, Israel fell. But Israel will recover! Yes, Israel was disobedient and obstinate. But Israel will receive a new heart! The Redeemer *will* "turn godlessness away from Jacob." He *will* "take away their sins." This people that has received more than its share of suffering will be blessed in its final end. It's time for the blessing to come! How great is the wisdom of God.

But there is a warning here as well.

If some of the [natural Israelite] branches have been broken off, and you [Gentiles], though a wild olive shoot, have been grafted in among the others [the Israelites who believed] and now share in the nourishing sap from the olive root [Israel], do not boast over those branches. If you do, consider this: You do not support the root, but the root supports you (Rom. 11:17-18).

How insensitive and arrogant for the grafted-in wild branches to boast over the natural branches.

May it be understood clearly and never forgotten: Gentile believers have been grafted into Israel's tree and they are nourished by the ancient Jewish root. (In this context, the root is not Jesus, although in other Scriptures Jesus is called the root of Jesse [see Isaiah 11:1], and the Vine from which we branch out [see John 15:1-9]. But when Paul speaks of the "root" in Romans 11:18, he seems to be referring to the patriarchs, the fathers of Israel.)[17] It is true that the natural branches "were broken off because of unbelief, and you [Gentile believers] stand by faith." But that is no reason for pride. On the contrary, "Do not be arrogant, but be afraid. For if God did not spare the natural branches, He will not spare you either" (Rom. 11:20-21).

Here is where the Church, which has been primarily Gentile since the second century, has made a big mistake. She has been guilty of boasting over the natural branches, forgetting her root and misinterpreting Israel's hardening.

Because she has boasted over the fallen Israelite branches, she has treated the Jewish people harshly, even glorying over Israel's suffering and pain. "After all, *they* were cut off to make room for me!" Because she has forgotten her Jewish root, she has added all kinds of alien customs to the faith, often overruling the Scriptures with traditions of men. "After all, we want to stay clear of all that *Old Testament* stuff. That's bondage!" Because she has misinterpreted Israel's hardening, which was only temporary and in part, she has proudly thought that God replaced His old people, Israel, with a new people, the Church. "All the blessings are now ours...forever. As for you Jews, to hell with your cursed race!"[18]

But the Church has not cursed Israel. The Church has cursed herself! The spiritual equation is simple: *To the extent that the Church has recognized her Jewish roots and the rightful place of Israel, the Church has had light.* The Dark Ages of the Church were the days of her greatest theological ignorance of Israel as well as the times of her most violent hostility against the Jews.

Paul's exhortation must be heard again:

Do not be *arrogant,* but be afraid....I do not want you to be *ignorant* of this mystery, brothers, so that you may not be *conceited...* (Rom. 11:20, 25)

Look at the strong words Paul uses: arrogant, ignorant, conceited. What a critically important subject for the Church to understand! Ignorance of God's purposes for Israel breeds conceit. And a conceited Church is a Church resisted by the Lord, for "God opposes the proud but gives grace to the humble" (James 4:6).

Unfortunately, many in the Body today still claim that it is the Church alone who is the true Israel. One well-known author has written at length and with great passion saying, "Wake up Church! You alone are Israel!" Although he states frankly in his book that Romans 11:26 "is somewhat of a problem," he goes on to say, "but I think the Lord has shown me how it will fit in." And what was the solution that the Lord supposedly showed him? "Israel" in Romans 11:25 is different than "Israel" in Romans 11:26![19] This also means that "Israel" in Romans 11:26 is different than "Israel" in Romans 9:3, 27, 31; 10:1, 16, 19, 21; 11:1-2, 7 and 11:11, as well as different from "Israel" in the rest of the New Testament! In spite of this brother's obvious sincerity, *God* did not tell him that.

One pastor went even further. Writing on Romans 11:28—"As far as the gospel is concerned, they are enemies on your account; but as far as election is concerned, they are loved on account of the patriarchs"—this pastor alleged that the word "they" in the first half of the verse refers to someone different than the word "they" in the second half of this same verse![20] This dear brother is willing to see the Jews as enemies of the gospel, but not as the elect of God, even if it means slicing the Word to pieces and engaging in a hopeless balancing act.

At this point I would like to make a proposal. Why don't we simply accept the obvious meaning of the text? Why don't we give up all our interpretive gymnastics?

God is looking for believers, not acrobats.

Chapter Fourteen
"Thou Shalt Not Steal"

For more than 1500 years, much of the Church has experienced an identity crisis. In the case of Jewish believers *who have been accepted as Jews by the rest of the Body,* the pressure came from outside. Other Jews told them they were no longer Jewish. Their unbelieving families held funeral services for them and called them *meshummadim,* "apostates" (literally, "destroyed ones"). They were viewed as defectors and base heretics by their mothers, fathers, brothers and sisters.[1]

But in the Lord they were secure. Not only was the New Testament their Book, but the whole Bible was uniquely theirs. The Law was their law and the Land was their land. They were spiritual children of Abraham as well as physical descendants. Moses, Elijah, David, Peter, James and John were all kinsmen after the flesh. The patriarchs and prophets were their own people.

In the case of Gentile believers things have been different. They have not had to deal so much with an external identity crisis as with an internal identity crisis. They are the newcomers, the late arrivals, the "spiritual immigrants," so to speak. Next to Jewish believers they have often felt insecure. (This insecurity, based on ignorance, has caused many of them to become arrogant.) In the Lord, of course, we are all equals, and all equals only.

> For there is no difference between Jew and Gentile—the same Lord is Lord of all and richly blesses all who call on Him (Rom. 10:12).

But not everyone has received this. Some Jewish believers have felt like *upper-class* citizens, in spite of what the Word says. (I speak here as a Jewish believer to my Jewish spiritual brothers.) We have been guilty of our own brand of pride. May the Lord have mercy on us lest our fleshly confidence completely undo us! We desperately need our non-Jewish brothers. We are not as much the fourth branch of Judaism as we are the Jewish part of the Church! It is only together with the rest of the Body that we will be perfect.

As for Gentile believers, some have felt like *second-class* citizens, in spite of what the Word says. For these insecure believers, it has not been enough to be spiritually grafted into Israel's tree and to "share in the nourishing sap from the olive root" (Rom. 11:17). It has not been enough to spiritually apply God's promises to Israel to their own lives. No! *They have stolen Israel's promises.* In the process, Satan has stolen from them.

Paul saw clearly from the Old Testament, his only Bible, that God had a place for the Gentiles in the Body right beside His people Israel. Paul did not randomly apply the glorious promises of *Israel's* future restoration to the Church. He saw instead that the Church—Messiah's Body, the Congregation of God—consisted of all believers from Israel and the nations.

Most religious Jews thought, and still think, that Jew and Gentile will not be united in one spiritual family in this age. Paul received a revelation: Since the Messianic age began when Jesus died, rose and ascended to heaven, the universal spiritual family also began:[2]

> For I tell you that Christ has become a servant of the Jews on behalf of God's truth, to confirm the promises made to the patriarchs so that the Gentiles may glorify God for His mercy, as it is written: "Therefore I will praise you among the Gentiles; I will sing hymns to Your name" [Ps. 18:49]. Again it says, "Rejoice, O Gentiles, with His people" [Deut. 32:43]. And again, "Praise the Lord, all you Gentiles, and sing praises to Him, all you peoples" [Ps. 117:1]" (Rom. 15:8-11).[3]

This is so important! Paul found the "mystery of the Church" hidden in Old Testament passages that spoke of the *Gentiles and Israel,* not Israel alone. He didn't simply take Israel's precious promises and prophecies and say, "Now this means the Church!" No. He quoted Deuteronomy: "Rejoice, O Gentiles, *with His people.*" Yet the largely Gentile Church has seemed to read these words as if they said, "Rejoice, O Gentiles, in place of His people."

Yes, Gentile believers, as well as Jewish believers, are the spiritual people of God. But *all* Jews are the natural people of God. And the Church has taken away God's promises to the Jews.

What is one of the Church's favorite verses of protection?

"No weapon forged against you will prevail, and you will refute every tongue that accuses you. This is the heritage of the servants of the LORD, and this is their vindication from Me," declares the LORD (Is. 54:17).

Now, all believers have the right to apply this verse to themselves. The end of the passage makes that clear. The Church as a whole can "claim" it. But no believer has the right to steal this promise from its rightful owner: Jerusalem!

Jerusalem? Yes! The promise starts in verse 11: "O afflicted city, lashed by storms and not comforted, I will build you with stones of turquoise, your foundations with sapphires." God is speaking to a *city*.

If anyone does attack you, it will not be My doing; whoever attacks you will surrender to you (54:15).

Although the word "city" does not occur in the Hebrew of Isaiah 54, the recipient of these comforting words is addressed throughout in the feminine because "city" in Hebrew is feminine![4]

Here is another verse the Church has stolen:

Can a mother forget the baby at her breast and have no compassion on the child she has borne? Though she may forget, I will not forget you (Is. 49:15).

Thank God for His faithfulness. He will not forget us! Neither will He forget the original recipient of this promise: *Zion!*

"But Zion said, 'The LORD has forsaken me, the LORD has forgotten me' " (49:14). God says absolutely not: "See, I have engraved you on the palms of My hands; *your walls* are ever before Me" (49:16).

He's talking to a city again! (The Hebrew is feminine, too.)

Of course, Zion doesn't refer only to the literal city of David. It represents the nation as a whole. As "mother Jerusalem" went, so went the nation. That much is understood. And in a *secondary sense,* Zion can apply to *all* the people of God.[5] But as people of God, let's be godly people. "Thou shalt not steal," He says. It is enough that the Church can embrace these glorious promises and partake in their nourishing sap. Why try to steal them entirely? How does that benefit the Church? Can't believers be secure enough to share?

In Isaiah 60:1-2, the prophet says:

Arise, shine, for your light has come, and the glory of the LORD rises upon you. See, darkness covers the earth and thick darkness is over the peoples, but the LORD rises upon you and His glory appears over you.

What a precious word! But who is being addressed? That's right; it's Zion again![6] (And, you guessed it, the Hebrew is feminine once more.)

Foreigners will rebuild your walls....Your gates will always stand open....The sons of your oppressors will come bowing before you; all who despise you will bow down at your feet and will call you *the City of the LORD, Zion of the Holy One of Israel* (60:10, 11, 15).

How Jerusalem needs these words!

Isaiah 62 is another classic chapter. In it the prophet pledges unceasing intercession. He will not give up in prayer. Who is he praying for?

> For Zion's sake I will not keep silent, for Jerusalem's sake I will not remain quiet, till her righteousness shines out like the dawn, her salvation like a blazing torch (62:1).

Go ahead and apply this to the Church and to the heavenly Mount Zion; just don't rob her earthly partner!

> I have posted watchmen on your walls, O Jerusalem; they will never be silent day or night. You who call on the LORD, give yourselves no rest, and give Him no rest till He establishes Jerusalem and makes her the praise of the earth (62:6-7).

That is something worth praying for![7]

There is a promise for Zion's land:

> No longer will they call you Deserted, or name your land Desolate. But you will be called Hephzibah [My delight is in her] and your land Beulah [Married]... (62:4).

There is a promise for Zion's people:

> They will be called the Holy People, the Redeemed of the LORD...(62:12).

And there is a promise for Zion herself:

> ...and you will be called Sought After, the City No Longer Deserted (62:12).

If Zion *primarily* means the Church, then where is Zion's land, what are its walls, and who are its people? We can make all the spiritual application we want. All believers have a spiritual right to the promises. But we must remember—they are *literally* true for Zion! Jerusalem's restoration will be glorious.

Isaiah 41:10 is another beloved Scripture:

So do not fear, for I am with you; do not be dismayed, for I am your God. I will strengthen you and help you; I will uphold you with My righteous right hand.

This time the Hebrew is masculine. The Lord is *not* speaking to the city. He's speaking here to the people!

But you, O Israel, My servant, Jacob, whom I have chosen, you descendants of Abraham my friend, I took you from the ends of the earth, from its farthest corners I called you. I said, "You are My servant"; I have chosen you and have not rejected you. So do not fear, for I am with you...(41:8-10).

That's the only reason the Jews are still here!

Let me speak now as a Jewish believer to my Gentile spiritual brothers. We are willing to share these promises with you. But please, save them for our natural brothers. They need them too! Soon they'll be grafted back in.

So the Church has broken the eighth commandment. The devil has broken it too. By convincing many believers that the promises to Israel no longer apply to the physical people, he has robbed these believers blind. They are unable to see the greatest fulfillment of prophecy in almost 2000 years: the restoration of national Israel! Who would have thought it possible?

The fact that the Jews have even survived this long is an outstanding miracle. No people has ever been completely displaced from its land and continued to exist for centuries *as a distinct people.* In spite of incredible odds, the Jews have done this. (Or, to put it more accurately, God has done this for the Jews.) But there is an even greater miracle than that. Not only have the Jews survived as a people, but after centuries of wandering, they have also returned to their ancestral homeland and made it their own country again. *The Bible said it would happen.* What the prophets spoke is literally true! And who would have believed that the language being spoken in this resurrected nation would again be Hebrew? Our God is an awesome God.

When Isaiah, Jeremiah and Ezekiel prophesied that their people would come out from Babylon and from the rest of the nations where they were scattered, these prophets were referring to the Jewish exile of their day. But their words were never fulfilled. Only some of the exiles returned, and their return was anything but glorious.[8] The majority of Jews remained scattered throughout the world, and in every generation the dispersion increased. Now, over the last 100 years, with amazing parallels to the restoration of the Church, God has said, "It's time!"

From 1948 to 1964 alone, Jews returned to the Land from Sweden, Belgium, Britain, Holland, Germany, Poland, France, Switzerland, Spain, Czechoslovakia, Austria, Hungary, Romania, Bulgaria, Greece, Yugoslavia, Italy, Turkey, Syria, Iraq, Iran, Afghanistan, Yemen, Aden, Egypt, Libya, Tunisia, Algeria, Morocco and Russia—to name just the closest nations! This is the hand of God.[9]

At this very time the gospel is being preached around the earth. Isaiah declared that in the day *the nations* rally to the Root of Jesse

> ...the Lord will reach out His hand *a second time* to reclaim the remnant [of His people] that is left from Assyria, from

Lower Egypt, from Upper Egypt, from Cush [Ethiopia; remember the Ethiopian Jews?], from Elam, from Babylonia, from Hamath and from the islands of the sea. He will raise a banner for the nations and gather the exiles of Israel; He will assemble the scattered people of Judah from the four quarters of the earth (Is. 11:10-12).

How similar this is to Romans 11:25-26! As God is reaping the world harvest of the Gentiles ("nations" in the Hebrew), He is regathering Israel's exiles from across the globe.[10] We are living in that "day."

Some Christians argue, "But the Jews returned to the Land in unbelief and the Law said they must first repent. So the modern state of Israel cannot be the fulfillment of prophecy."[11]

But that is only part of what the Scriptures say. According to the Word, if the Jewish people, scattered throughout the world, would turn to God in repentance, the Lord would bring them back to their land (Deut. 30). Because they did not repent as a nation, they were without a homeland for over nineteen centuries. But a time comes when God says, "Enough!" A time comes when He must act for His own name's sake, when He cannot hold back any longer.

...This is what the Sovereign LORD says: "It is not for your sake, O house of Israel, that I am going to do these things, but for the sake of My holy name, which you have profaned among the nations....For I will take you out of the nations; I will gather you from all the countries and bring you back into your own land. I will sprinkle clean water on you, and you will be clean....I will give you a new heart and put a new spirit in you; I will remove from you your heart of stone and give you a heart of flesh....I want you to know that I am not doing this for your sake, declares the Sovereign LORD. Be ashamed and disgraced for your conduct, O house of Israel" (Ezek. 36:22-32).

The physical restoration comes first, but not because of Israel's deeds. The spiritual restoration follows, once they are again in the Land.

The spiritual did not come first, but the natural, and after that the spiritual (1 Cor. 15:46).

The natural has already come; the spiritual will surely follow.

Do you see the devil's strategy? He has robbed many Christians of the natural so that they will not believe God for the spiritual. When the Lord performed the greatest miracle of modern times, restoring the nation of Israel—using human means in the process, as He always does—the devil was right there to say, "That's not a miracle! That's not God! That's just a natural political development." How Satan *hates* what God does! I'm sure he was whispering the same lies in the ears of many exiled Jews when Cyrus said they could return home in 538 B.C.E. "It's just politics! Don't give the glory to God. And what's wrong with Babylon anyway?"

Today, when a supernatural exodus is taking place out of what was formerly the Soviet Union and Russian Jews are *flooding* into Israel, when Jeremiah's prophecy of an exodus greater than the exodus from Egypt (Jer. 16:14-15; 23:7-8) is approaching fulfillment,[12] the devil is really screaming. "This has nothing to do with the Bible!"

Why is he getting so desperate? Well, the devil always seeks to quench our faith. He constantly tries to deny the works of the Lord and to convince us they are not real.

He'll do this with every genuine miracle every time one occurs. He always has an anti-supernatural explanation! But when it comes to Israel, Satan is really scrambling. The stakes are infinitely higher.

It was easier for him to deny God's promises to the Jewish people before 1948. Before then, it was not as hard for him to mislead the Church into thinking that it had replaced natural Israel. But once the nation was physically reborn it became more difficult. And Satan knows what's coming. There is a tremendous battle of faith immediately ahead. *It is for the salvation of the Jewish people.* The faith-filled prayers of the Church are essential.

Now stop and think for a moment: We have reason to be encouraged; so the enemy is trying to discourage us. God said that the nation of Israel would have a physical rebirth. That has happened, just as He said! He spoke of the places from which He would regather His scattered people. That is happening, just as He said! And He promised that when He brought His people back into the Land, they would have a spiritual rebirth too. That will happen, just as He said! As surely as Israel exists, Israel will be saved.

The Lord is raising His voice and shouting, "My children, believe My Word!" Satan is screeching hysterically, "Don't believe it, it's not the Word!" And just why is the devil trying so frantically to steal our faith for the salvation of the Jewish people? He knows *exactly* why.

Do we?

Chapter Fifteen
A Diabolical Plan

With every fiber of his depraved, sinister being, Satan despises the Jews. He hates them with a perfect hatred. Their total destruction is his goal. *He* is the author of the spirit of anti-Semitism. There is no other way to explain the venomous hostility that has been hurled against the Jews by so many people in so many countries for so many years.[1]

Why the Jews? That is a question that has been asked countless times, and countless answers have been given. Some people have said that Christianity itself is the chief cause of anti-Semitism, since the Church has accused the Jews of deicide (killing God), thus falling forever from grace.[2] But this theory does not explain the presence of anti-Semitism in non-Christian countries like Japan or Iran, nor does it account for the fact that anti-Semitism existed *before* Christianity began.[3] Jerusalem and the Jewish people were on the devil's hit list long before Jesus came into the world! (Read Ezra 4:12-16 and the Book of Esther for some good examples.)

Some scholars have argued that the Jews have suffered because every generation needs to find a scapegoat. When things go wrong, human beings tend to blame others rather than take the blame themselves.[4] But this really begs the question rather than answers it. Why are the *Jews* the universal scapegoats? Why have *they* been blamed for the Black Plague and the spread of AIDS, for economic difficulties in communist Russia and capitalist America, for creating problems in the Catholic Church and the Protestant world? Why always the Jews?[5]

Could it be that the *Jews themselves* are the reason for anti-Semitism? Are Jews more obnoxious and despicable than everyone else?[6] Hardly! We Jews may have a reputation for being stubborn, contentious, money-hungry and proud, but those qualities are shared by plenty of Gentiles! And there are more than enough kind and gentle Jews all over the world. Even if we Jews are sometimes stiff-necked, this would only account for some of the negative sentiment toward us; but it could not possibly explain the irrational, murderous hatred that we have encountered everywhere we have resided for centuries.[7]

Some have argued that the reason the Jews have been so universally persecuted is because of the uniqueness of *Judaism.*[8] Religious Jews claim to be the chosen people, and that insults the rest of the world. Jewish laws and traditions make them a separated people, and that offends their Gentile neighbors. Jews believe that there is only one true God, a holy God with high standards and laws, and this accuses the rest of the world of idolatry and transgression. Nobody likes to be accused! And because Jewish customs are good and Jewish study habits exceptional, Jews tend to be extremely successful in virtually everything they put their hand to, making everybody else jealous.

Yet even this theory, with all its apparent truth, has holes.[9] Why are *secular* Jews hated too? Why are *ordinary* Jews persecuted, average Jews who have become ordinary members of society? And, if Jews have been persecuted because of their ethical monotheism, why have *Muslims* often persecuted Jews? Also, Muslims believe in one God who has high standards and laws, and they have traditions that make them separate. Yet Muslims have not been universally persecuted!

No, it is not merely Judaism's uniqueness that has brought about worldwide anti-Semitism. The fact is, if traditional Judaism were correct, it should have produced worldwide Jewish exaltation and honor, similar to the days of David and Solomon. According to the Torah, obedience to God's laws would bring blessing to Israel *in this world.* Yet when we read the agonizing history of the Jewish people, we see century after century of covenant curse, *not* blessing. Just compare Deuteronomy 28 with the story of Israel. The conclusion is unavoidable: Jewish history does not primarily describe the events of a people enjoying the covenant blessings.[10]

Of course, statements such as these infuriate Jewish leaders and scholars, and I fully understand why![11] This has been the "Christian" position for fifteen ugly centuries. And referring to Jewish people as being in any way under God's curse seems to move us back into the Dark Ages of

the Church instead of forward into times of mutual understanding and enlightenment. But the Church's fatal error
was not in believing that the Jewish people were temporarily under divine disfavor for rejecting the Messiah. No. That
could only produce compassion and sensitivity for the
Jewish people. The Church erred fatally by thinking that
God's disfavor toward Israel was permanent. It was His
choosing of Israel that was permanent! *Yet as the chosen
people, Israel has suffered greatly because of its national
disobedience.*

Is there any other conclusion that can be reached from
an honest reading of the Hebrew Bible? Isn't the Mosaic
covenant clear? It is one thing to point to examples of
righteous *individuals* who seem to suffer inexplicably. It is
another thing entirely to say that national, obedient Israel
could suffer inexplicably. God's covenant with His people
was absolute: National obedience would bring about national blessing.[12] Yet the times of greatest Jewish suffering
have sometimes been the times of greatest national ad-
herence to Judaism![13]

If the leaders of traditional Jewry *were* correct in rejecting the claims of Jesus the Messiah and taking a decided
stand against Him, they should have been *favored* by God
for *refusing* Jesus. That would be in keeping with the terms
of the Mosaic covenant! Instead, Jewish suffering only *increased* after the Messiah was disavowed.[14]

Then is the whole reason for anti-Semitism simply
Jewish disobedience? That would be a gross and unjust exaggeration.[15] Hatred against the Jews has been too intense,

too cruel, too universal, too destructive to be explained in terms of divine punishment alone. Yossel Rakover's Holocaust prayer says it so painfully well:

> You say, I know, that we have sinned, O Lord. It must surely be true! And therefore we are punished? I can understand that too! But I should like You to tell me whether *there is any sin in the world deserving such a punishment as the punishment we have received!*[16]

Anti-Semitism has clearly overstepped the bounds of heavenly judgment and chastisement. The origins of Jew-hatred *are* supernatural—but not from above.

No, it is not simply Christianity, or the need to find a scapegoat, or negative aspects of Jewish personality, or the pattern of Jewish success, or the uniqueness of Judaism or divine chastisement that is wholly responsible for anti-Semitism. None of these theories totally works, although there is truth in each one of them.

In reality, there is only one way to explain anti-Semitism: *The devil hates the Jews, and his demented nature is revealed in his treatment of the Jewish people.* While many other nations and groups have felt the fury of his wrath, none have felt it so often, so consistently and so powerfully as have the Jews.

The Holocaust is inexplicable from a solely natural point of view. There had to be a greater force at work, inciting and provoking the Nazis. The words of Adolf Eichmann toward the end of World War II defy human description:

I shall leap into my grave laughing, because the feeling that
I have the deaths of five million people on my conscience
will be for me a source of extraordinary satisfaction.[17]

The Nazis were *entertained* by Jewish suffering and
torment.

Writes Elie Wiesel:

Imagine: the chief rabbi of the town forced by German officers to clean the pavement, to sweep it with his beard. And
all around, proud soldiers, warriors puffed up with their vic-
tories, slapped their thighs in merriment. Imagine: a distinguished officer, a man of good family, orders Jewish
children to run, like rabbits, and then he takes out his revolv-
er and begins shooting at the terrified living targets, scattering them, mowing them down. Imagine: no, let us not
imagine anymore. In those days, the executioners had more
imagination than their victims.[18]

They were satanically creative. Wiesel continues:

They used every science and technique. Among them were
philosophers and psychologists, doctors and artists, experts
in management and specialists in poisoning the mind.[19]

These were all driven, all impelled, all given over to the
humiliation, degradation and extermination of the Jews.
Only yesterday they were neighbors and friends!

When the Nazis murdered all the patients of the Lodz
ghetto hospitals they threw *newborn babies* out of upper-
story hospital windows. Precious Jewish infants were splat-
tered on the pavement! But for one teenaged SS soldier this
was not enough. He asked permission—and was granted
permission—to catch the falling babes on his *bayonet.*[20] Is
there no limit to hell's depravity?

The horrors of the Chmielnicki massacres in Eastern Europe, taking over 100,000 Jewish lives from 1648 to 1656, must have been demonically inspired. What else would motivate peasant mobs to tear open the bellies of pregnant women, cut off their hands to render them helpless, and then place living cats within their bellies—just because they were Jewesses?[21]

If the devil himself, *the father of lies,* is not ultimately responsible for anti-Semitism, then why have so many people believed such *ludicrous* anti-Jewish lies, lies that in any other context would be laughable? It is not only the ignorant and unlearned who have been duped, but it is political and social leaders, spiritual and intellectual giants, who have also been deceived.[22]

Why was a brilliant (and anti-Christian) philosopher like Voltaire so harshly anti-Semitic? According to Voltaire, the Jews' crime was "None other than that of being born."

He wrote:

You have surpassed all nations in impertinent fables, in bad conduct, and in barbarism. You deserve to be punished, for this is your destiny.[23]

Why did a pious monk like Bernard of Clairvaux speak with such antagonism toward the very people he sought to protect?[24] Why did a gifted *composer* like Richard Wagner believe that the Jewish race was "the born enemy of pure humanity and all that is noble in man"?[25] (Jews have *excelled* in music and the arts.) Why did the renowned historian Professor Arnold Toynbee have a severe blind spot when it came to the Jews? He claimed that Jewish history since the birth of Christianity and Islam was "a classic example of perversity" and that Jewish Zionists were "disciples of the Nazis."[26]

Voltaire the deist philosopher, Bernard the Catholic saint, Wagner the operatic composer, Toynbee the world historian (they are merely a representative sampling[27]) were all poisoned by the devil's gall. It infected their entire system!

If the evil one himself is not ultimately responsible for anti-Semitism, then why have Jewish *cemeteries* been desecrated in Canada, London, France, Italy, Czechoslovakia and Israel, all in 1990?[28] Who inspired the young French vandals to dig up the corpse of a recently buried eighty-year-old Jewish man and violate him with a parasol? *Acts like this are birthed in the pit.*

Although other peoples have been occasionally subjected to torture and brutality, it has been common for the Jew. In fact, in every century it has been *the norm.* Raymond Barre, the former Prime Minister of France, once made a statement that typifies the world's view of the Jews. He "described the bombing of a Paris synagogue as an event which, 'while aimed at Jews going to synagogue, hit innocent Frenchmen.' "[29] In other words, those Jews deserve what they get! *Anti-Semitism is out of control.*

Close your eyes for a moment and feel the pulsating rhythm of the "Hate-the-Jew" song as it captivates the nations of the world. The Muslims are dancing to its beat. Communist China is familiar with its tune. Europe often moves to its tempo. Some Americans are humming along. The "Church" has written the lyrics. And Satan is orchestrating it all!

Islam thrives on hatred of Israel.[30] Arab nations eagerly await Jihad (holy war). There must be a scapegoat for the ongoing Middle East crisis, and Israel will certainly be blamed. Why should Asia and Africa side with Israel? Why should South America unite with the Jews? What will keep the U.S.A. faithful? Why should Russia befriend a nation that is an enemy of its Middle Eastern friends? The devil is convincing the world that Israel is the problem. It's time to get rid of the Jews!

Why does Satan so passionately despise the Jews? For one thing, it is a reflection of his hatred for God. The Jews are God's chosen people! By hurting them he seeks to hurt the Lord and take revenge for his own sentence of death. His effort to annihilate the Jews is also an attempt to discredit the Lord, since He has sworn in His Word that they will never be destroyed. If Israel ceases to exist as a distinct people, then God did not, or could not, keep His promise. That would mean that He was either powerless or that He had lied!

But there is a another reason the devil despises the Jews: *The salvation of Israel means the return of Jesus, the resurrection of the righteous, the revival of the Church and the restoration of the earth.*[31] The fulfillment of the Jews' destiny will seal the devil's doom. Yes, "the God of peace will soon crush Satan under your feet" (Rom. 16:20)...and he is beginning to squirm! The time to favor Israel is upon us and Satan is quaking with fear.

The countdown has begun.

Chapter Sixteen

Life from the Dead

Hosanna to the Son of David! Blessed is He Who comes in the name of the Lord! Hosanna in the highest!

With these words of excitement and anticipation the crowds greeted Jesus as He made His way to Jerusalem (Matt. 21:9).[1] "This is the day of redemption! This is the day of deliverance! This is the day we have longed for! Messiah has come to free us! He has come, He has finally come!" Less than one week later the Lord of glory was nailed to a cross, and even His disciples forsook Him.

But very soon He will come again—to Jerusalem. At that time the scene will be repeated. *But He will remain in heaven until Jerusalem welcomes Him back.* That is how it must be!

King David fled from Jerusalem when his son Absalom stole the throne. But after Absalom was killed, it was time for David's return.

Throughout the tribes of Israel, the people were all arguing with each other, saying, "The king delivered us from the hand of our enemies; he is the one who rescued us from the

hand of the Philistines. But now he has fled the country because of Absalom; and Absalom, whom we anointed to rule
over us, has died in battle. So why do you say nothing about
bringing the king back?" (2 Sam. 19:9-10).

But David wanted something more and he sent this message through the priests:

…"*Ask the elders of Judah*, 'Why should you be the last to
bring the king back to his palace, since what is being said
throughout Israel has reached the king at his quarters? *You
are my brothers, my own flesh and blood. So why should you
be the last to bring back the king?*' " (2 Sam. 19:11-12).

These words have prophetic meaning!

Believers throughout the world are crying out,
"Maranatha! O Lord, come!" People from every nation are
praying for the Messiah's return. But He is waiting for
something very important to Him. *He must be received by
His brothers.* Until then, He will not come. Jerusalem,
standing for Israel and the Jewish people, must welcome
Him back. Our Jewish Savior sends this message through
the Church: "Ask My Jewish people, 'You are My brothers,
My own flesh and blood. So why should you be the last to
bring back the King?' " Israel, the world is waiting for
you![2]

John said that when the Lord comes back with the
clouds, "every eye will see Him" (Rev. 1:7). But Jesus said
to Jerusalem:

Look, your house is left to you desolate. For I tell you, *you
will not see Me again* until you say, "Blessed is He Who
comes in the name of the Lord" (Matt. 23:38-39).[3]

He must be received as the Messiah *by His very own people* before He will return to Jerusalem. Only the family of David can welcome the Son of David back to the City of David.

This simple conclusion is inescapable: If *every eye* will see Him when He returns, and if Jerusalem *will not see Him* until she welcomes Him back, then *no eye* will see Him until Jerusalem receives Him! *All eyes,* worldwide, are already on Jerusalem. Soon they'll focus on Jerusalem's King!

Peter brought a similar message to the Temple crowds just days after Jesus had ascended:

> Repent, then, and turn to God, so that your sins may be wiped out, that times of refreshing may come from the Lord, and that He may send the Messiah, who has been appointed for you—even Jesus. He must remain in heaven until the time comes for God to restore everything, as He promised long ago through His holy prophets (Acts 3:19-21).

This is what Peter is saying: "Jerusalem, Jewish leadership, people of Israel, repent and turn to God...*that He may send the Messiah.*" Jewish repentance will bring Jesus back![4] *But the Church must repent first, before it will be Israel's turn.*

There is a principle that cannot be violated: We must make restitution for the past if we want our present and future to be blessed.[5] There is a clear example in the Word:

> During the reign of David, there was a famine for three successive years; so David sought the face of the LORD. The LORD said, "It is on account of Saul and his blood-stained

house; it is because he put the Gibeonites to death" (2 Sam. 21:1).

But David wasn't guilty! He wasn't related to Saul; he certainly wasn't responsible for Saul's sinful acts. And David was totally ignorant of what had been done. Yet the whole nation suffered just the same. The blood of the Gibeonites had to be avenged, and David was the only one who could do it. This is how it had to be. Only Saul's successor, God's anointed representative, could set the record straight. So after David made amends, "God answered prayer in behalf of the land" (2 Sam. 21:14).

In the very same way, *the Church will never completely see its way out of spiritual famine until it repents for shedding Jewish blood.*

"But I'm not guilty!" you say. Neither was David! Yet who else could right the wrongs done to the Gibeonites by the former king of Israel if not the present king himself? And who else can right the wrongs done to the Jewish people by the Church in former years if not the present Church itself?

"But I'm not related!" you say. "The Church that persecuted Israel wasn't the true Church." David wasn't directly related to Saul either! Yet as God's present representative, only he could repair what his carnal predecessor had done. It is the same with the Church and the Jewish people: We who are the spiritual representatives of the Lord Jesus must repair what our carnal predecessors have done in His name. And to be perfectly honest, it is not only the outward, carnal, hypocritical Church that sinned so greatly against Israel. There were, and still are, many true believers who have stumbled and fallen here.[6] You may be related after all!

"But I'm ignorant!" you say. Not anymore, my friend. Your only response, my only response, the Church's only response, is to fall on our faces and repent, to fast and ask for cleansing, to purge ourselves of all anti-Semitic strains and to *unconditionally* love the Jews—every single one.[7] Then we can tell them the truth: the truth about our shameful past, and the truth about their glorious future, if they will turn to Jesus the King. After that, "God will answer prayer in behalf of the Church." Incredible refreshing will come! *Israel's re-ingrafting will be glorious.*

Listen to Paul's words again:

> ...Did they stumble so as to fall beyond recovery? Not at all! Rather, because of their transgression, salvation has come to the Gentiles to make Israel envious (Rom. 11:11).

The day will come when Gentile believers will make Israel envious! The results will be almost inexpressible.

> [For] if their transgression means riches for the world, and their loss means riches for the Gentiles, how much greater riches will their fullness bring! (Rom. 11:12).

What an extraordinary word!

Today, there are men and women across the globe who are children of the living God, the spiritual seed of Abraham, joint-heirs with the Messiah, recipients of eternal life, blood-washed, Spirit-filled, consecrated saints *as a result of Israel's transgression.* How much greater riches will Israel's fullness bring!

At this very moment, a continuous stream of praise ascends to heaven in more than *2500* languages, and angels shout for joy as sinners repent worldwide *as a result of Israel's loss.* How much greater riches will Israel's fullness bring!

The Good News has been preached on every continent and Buddhist priests, animist witch doctors, Muslim clerics, Hindu devotees, atheist professors, masses of humanity from all walks of life—both terrorists and those whom they terrorized, oppressors and those whom they oppressed, deceivers and those whom they deceived, "a great multitude that no one could count, from every nation, tribe, people and language" (Rev. 7:9)[8]—have been harvested into the Kingdom *as a result of Israel's disobedience.* How much greater riches will Israel's fullness bring! And yet there is more!

> For if their rejection is the reconciliation of the world, what will their acceptance be but life from the dead (Rom. 11:15).

Life from the dead at last!

Paul is not just teaching that the Church will be refreshed, that ancient hostilities will cease, that unprecedented outpouring will come, that revival will sweep through many nations, that all the unreached will be reached. No! He is promising even more.

If Israel's *rejection* meant the reconciliation of the world, then Israel's *acceptance* must mean something far greater. It will mean *the resurrection of those reconciled,* literally, life from the dead![9] And Israel *will* be accepted! For "if the part of the dough offered as firstfruits is holy, then the whole batch is holy; if the root is holy, so are the branches" (Rom. 11:16). God will save the whole batch!

The Jewish people will welcome back their Messiah with the words, "Blessed is He Who comes in the name of the Lord!" And when Jesus descends

> in a flash, in the twinkling of an eye...*the dead will be raised imperishable, and we will be changed* (1 Cor. 15:52).

Death will suddenly come to an end!

> For the Lord Himself will come down from heaven, with a loud command, with the voice of the archangel and with the trumpet call of God, and the dead in Christ will rise first. After that, we who are still alive and are left will be caught up together with them in the clouds to meet the Lord in the air. *And so we will be with the Lord forever* (1 Thess. 4:16-17)—

when Israel turns back!

> On that day His feet will stand on the Mount of Olives, east of Jerusalem....On that day there will be no light, no cold or frost....When evening comes, there will be light. On that day living water will flow out from Jerusalem....On that day there will be one LORD, and His name the only name (Zech. 14:4-9)—

when Israel calls on Yeshua!

On that day, they will look on the One they have pierced

> ...and they will mourn for Him as one mourns for an only child, and grieve bitterly for Him as one grieves for a

firstborn son. On that day the weeping in Jerusalem will be great.... (Zech. 12:10-11)—

when Israel recognizes its Crucified King! *But they first must see His image in us.*

* * *

One day...by God's grace may it be very soon!

...the LORD Almighty will prepare a feast of rich food for all peoples, a banquet of aged wine—the best of meats and the finest of wines. On this mountain [Jerusalem!] He will destroy the shroud that enfolds all peoples, the sheet that covers all nations; He will swallow up death forever. The Sovereign LORD will wipe away the tears from all faces; He will remove the disgrace of His people [the Jews!] from all the earth...(Is. 25:6-8)—

but first the Church must weep.

Let us cry and mourn *today,* so that Israel will repent *tomorrow.* Then Jesus will return, death will be no more and suffering will cease...forever. And when the weeping of sorrow finally mingles with the pent-up weeping of joy, Almighty God will reach out His hand and wipe away every tear. No more gas chambers, no more inquisitions, no more crusades, no more hatred, no more sin...forever.

And the ransomed of the LORD
will return.
They will enter Zion with singing;
everlasting joy will crown their heads.
Gladness and joy will overtake them,
and sorrow and sighing
will flee away (Is. 35:10)—

when the Lord makes all of us one!

Oh, the depth of the riches
of the wisdom and knowledge of God!
How unsearchable His judgments,
and His paths beyond tracing out!
"Who has known the mind of the Lord?
Or who has been His counselor?
Who has ever given to God,
that God should repay Him?"
For from Him and through Him
and to Him are all things.
To Him be the glory forever!
Amen! (Rom. 11:33-36).

Let the people of God say, "Amen!"

Notes

Preface

1. Reprinted in the *New York Times,* May 9, 1985, my emphasis, and quoted by Alan Gould, ed., *What Did They Think of the Jews?* (Northvale, NJ: Jason Aronson, 1991), p. 540.

2. Deut. 4:10, 5:15, 7:18, 8:2, 9:7, 24:9, 25:17, 25:19. These are just some of the "remembers" in Deuteronomy, not to mention the rest of the Old Testament. Concerning Amalek, "the LORD said to Moses, '*Write this on a scroll as something to be remembered...*' " (Exod. 17:14).

3. Edward H. Flannery, *The Anguish of the Jews: Twenty-three Centuries of Anti-Semitism,* (New York/Mahwah: Paulist Press, 1985), p. 1, my emphasis.

4. Meir Simcha Sokolovsky, *Prophecy and Providence* (English translation Jerusalem/New York: Feldheim Publishers, 1991), pp. 71f.

5. I personally believe that there is a special relationship between African Americans and Jews: Both are liberated slaves; both have been (and still are) persecuted minorities; both have a special "soul"—a unique personality and gifting. One day I believe we will see that we desperately need

each other! All of this makes the recent events in New York City all the more tragic.

6. All this is documented throughout this book.

7. It is important to state at the beginning of this study that I am *not* accusing the contemporary Christian authors with whom I disagree of being motivated by an anti-Semitic spirit. I believe most of them are sincere seekers who, I hope, will one day repudiate their current positions regarding the Jewish people. If any of them are, in fact, anti-Semitic, their writings will speak for themselves.

As far as the Jewish readership is concerned, I know some will be offended over my insistence that *Jewish people need Jesus.* To some Jews even *this* is an anti-Semitic position! But as a Jew who has received mercy through the atoning death of Jesus, Yeshua, the Jewish Messiah, it is only right that I long to see the rest of my people receive His mercy, too. Whoever reads these pages with an open heart will have to acknowledge that it is possible to have an *unconditional* love for the Jewish people while believing that they, like everyone else, need to embrace Jesus as Messiah and Lord.

Chapter One—The Final Solution

The horrors of the Holocaust, Hitler's "final solution" for the Jews, are indescribable. The narrative I have written in this chapter is based on actual survivors' accounts and seeks to recapture some of the countless agonies experienced by millions of the Nazis' victims, Jew and Gentile alike. For more information, see the Bibliographical Supplement to Chapter One.

1. Primo Levi, *Survival in Auschwitz* (trans. by Stuart Woolf, New York: Collier, 1961, originally published in Eng. as *If This Is a Man*), p. 112.

2. Miklos Nyiszli, *Auschwitz. A Doctor's Eyewitness Account* (trans. by Tibere Kremer and Richard Seaver, New York: Fawcett Crest, 1960), pp. 49-50.

Chapter Two—A Terrible, Tragic Past

1. Dennis Prager and Joseph Telushkin, *Why the Jews? The Reason for Antisemitism* (New York: Simon & Schuster, 1983), p. 104. The following account, so sickening, yet so typical, describing events that occurred in Dzialoszyce, Poland, September 2, 1942, graphically illustrates the depth of "Christian" hatred of the Jew that helped make the Holocaust possible. The reader should pay careful attention to the italicized paragraph toward the end of the quote:

"...The old, the sick, pregnant women and small children, two thousand innocent Jewish souls, were shot and brutally thrown into [freshly dug] graves, one on top of the other. Many of them were still alive! For most of the children they didn't even waste a bullet. They were just thrown in alive. And together with those who were only wounded, finished their lives under the pressure of the human mass.

"The next morning, a few of the wounded were able to crawl out of the graves and managed to walk a few metres, but died shortly thereafter....

"The larger grave contained a thousand bodies, and the two smaller graves contained five hundred bodies each. We learned of this massacre from the Polish police themselves. They told [our friend] Moshe Hersh about it in great detail, because they themselves had taken part in that slaughter.

"*On the following Sunday, they went to church with their families, as if nothing had happened. They suffered no guilt feelings. After all, they were only murdering Jews, with the blessing of their priests, who inflamed them from their pulpits on Sundays*" (Martin Rosenblum, quoted in Martin Gilbert, *The Holocaust: A History of the Jews During the Second World War* [New York: Henry Holt, 1985], p. 445, my emphasis).

Rosenblum was the only member of his family to survive. This is the account of his last minutes with his family, before he and some schoolmates escaped from the town:

"It is impossible to describe the agony of those few moments before we parted. I will never forget the wise eyes of my father and the tears of my mother when we embraced for the last time. In my wildest dreams I would never have imagined that I was parting from my whole family forever, never to see them again" (*Ibid.*, p. 444).

2. Prager and Telushkin, *ibid.*, p. 108.

3. Raul Hillberg, *The Destruction of the European Jews* (one volume edition; New York: Holmes & Meier, 1985), pp. 7f.

4. For a balanced assessment of early (rabbinic) Jewish hostility toward Jewish and/or Gentile believers in Jesus, see Edward Flannery, *The Anguish of the Jews*, pp. 34-46, with notes on pp. 303-305.

5. Quoted in Malcolm Hay, *The Roots of Christian Anti-Semitism* (New York: Liberty Press, 1981), p. 27.

6. *Ibid.*, pp. 27-28.

7. *Ibid.*, p. 32.

8. *Ibid.*, p. 21.

9. According to Flannery, "One chronicler, Guibert of Nogent, (1053-1124) reported the crusaders of Rouen as saying: 'We desire to combat the enemies of God in the East; but we have under our eyes the Jews, a race more inimical to God than all the others. We are doing this whole thing backwards.' " And so, "Great, ill-organized hordes of nobles, knights, monks, and peasants—'God wills it' on their lips as they set off to free the Holy Land from the Muslim infidel—suddenly turned on the Jews." (*Anguish of the Jews*, pp. 90-91).

10. Prager and Telushkin, *Why the Jews?*, p. 200, n. 3. Note also p. 18: "In the Russian Empire during the nineteenth and

twentieth centuries, mass beatings and murders of Jews were so common that a word, *pogrom*, was coined to describe such incidents."

11. Hay, *Christian Anti-Semitism*, pp. 54-56. Hay's comment on Bernard's final words, *viz.*, that the Jews had the devil as their father, bears repeating: "These are the words reported in the Gospel according to St. John (VIII:44) to have been addressed by Christ to a few individual Jews during a discussion in the Temple at Jerusalem. St. Bernard, following the usual custom of Christian commentators, applied them to the whole Jewish people, not only at that time, but for all time to come. In 1941, [Nazi leader] Julius Streicher adopted the same dialectical device when he recommended 'the extermination of that people whose father is the Devil.' " (*Ibid.*, p. 56) In other words, while the New Testament itself is not anti-Semitic, its statements were utilized in later anti-Semitic polemics.

Prager and Telushkin, however, contend that according to the New Testament, all Jews have the devil as their father: "A Jew who accepts Jesus as the Messiah and as divine is no longer a Jew, but a Christian. The New Testament passage [John 8:44], therefore, refers to all Jews as children of the Devil." (*Why the Jews?*, p. 93, bottom). But this statement cannot be accepted, since from a first-century, New Testament perspective, it would be incorrect to state that "A Jew who accepts Jesus as the Messiah and as divine is no longer a Jew, but a Christian." At the time of the writing of the Gospel of John, Jewish followers of Jesus were regarded as Jews, even by their opponents. See Lawrence H. Schiffman, *Who Was a Jew? Rabbinic and Halakhic Perspectives on the Jewish-Christian Schism* (Hoboken, NJ: Ktav, 1985), as well as Chapter Five and Chapter Eight of this book.

As for Jesus' words: "You are of your father the devil," we must remember that according to the New Testament, *everyone*, Jew and Gentile alike, who denies the lordship of

Jesus or continues to live in sin is outside the family of God, and thus is "of the devil....under the control of the evil one" (1 John 3:8, 5:19). Paul's mission *to the Gentiles* was to turn them "from the power of Satan to God" (Acts 26:18). The New Testament is no more anti-Semitic than it is anti-Gentile! It should also be noted that if negative statements about Israel and the Jewish people are the criterion for anti-Semitism, then the Hebrew Scriptures themselves (often quoting the very words of God!) are even more "anti-Semitic" than the New Testament (see, e.g., passages like Ezekiel 2:3-8, 3:7 and Isaiah 30:9).

12. *Ibid.,* p. 56.

13. *Ibid.,* p. 57.

14. See Joshua Trachtenberg, *The Devil and the Jews: The Medieval Conception of the Jew and its Relation to Modern Antisemitism* (New Haven: Yale Univ. Press, 1943).

15. Hay, *ibid.,* pp. 76 and 81.

16. *Ibid.,* p. 86.

17. *Ibid.,* p. 87.

18. Martin Luther, *That Jesus Christ Was Born a Jew,* reprinted in Frank Ephraim Talmage, ed., *Disputation and Dialogue: Readings in the Jewish-Christian Encounter* (New York: Ktav/Anti-Defamation League of B'nai B'rith, 1975), p. 33.

19. Martin Luther, *Concerning the Jews and Their Lies,* reprinted in Talmage, Disputation and Dialogue, pp. 34-36.

20. This recent Lutheran statement is typical: "We cannot accept or condone the violent verbal attacks that the Reformer made against the Jews. The sins of Luther's anti-Jewish remarks and the violence of his attacks on the Jews must be acknowledged with deep distress, and all occasion for similar sin in the present or the future must be removed from

our churches...Lutherans of today refuse to be bound by all
of Luther's utterances against the Jews" (from The World
Lutheran Federation, 1984 [celebrating the 500th anniver-
sary of Martin Luther's birth], quoted in Shlomo Hizak,
Building or Breaking [Jerusalem Center for Biblical Studies
and Research, 1985], p. 32). For an analysis of the impact
and meaning of the Catholic Church's 1965 statement,
Nostra Aetate ("In Our Time"), see Eugene J. Fischer, A.
James Rudin and Marc H. Tannebaum, eds., *Twenty Years of
Jewish-Catholic Relations* (New York/Mahwah: Paulist
Press, 1986).

21. Gerhard Kittel, from his book *Die Judenfrage* ("The Jewish
    Question"), quoted in Charlotte Klein, *Anti-Judaism in
    Christian Theology* (trans. by Edward Quinn, Philadelphia:
    Fortress Press, 1978), pp. 12-13.

22. Robert P. Ericksen, *Theologians Under Hitler* (New Haven:
    Yale Univ. Press, 1985), pp. 76 and 74.

23. At the time that the Nazis forced the Jews to wear a yellow
    star on their clothes, "An awkard situation was created for
    the churches when baptized Jews with stars turned up for
    services....The representatives of the Evangelical-Lutheran
    church in seven provinces invoked the teachings of Martin
    Luther to declare that racially Jewish Christians had no
    place and no rights in a German Evangelical church" (Raul
    Hillberg, *The Destruction of the European Jews,* p. 58).

24. I would recommend the reading of Malcom Hay's book,
    quoted often in this chapter, for all those wanting further
    evidence of the shameful heritage of "Christian" anti-
    Semitism.

Chapter Three—A Blessed and Beautiful Stream

1. For the Puritans and Israel, see Iain H. Murray, *The Puritan
   Hope. Revival and the Interpretation of Prophecy* (Carlisle,
   PA: Banner of Truth, 1971); for edifying surveys of Puritan

thought and piety, see D. Martyn Lloyd-Jones, *The Puritans: Their Origins and Successors* (Carlisle, PA: Banner of Truth, 1981); Leland Ryken, *Worldly Saints. The Puritans as They Really Were* (Grand Rapids: Zondervan, 1986); J. I. Packer, *A Quest for Godliness. The Puritan Vision of the Christian Life* (Wheaton: Crossway Books, 1990).

2. John Owen, quoted in *A Puritan Golden Treasury*, compiled by I. D. E. Thomas (Carlisle, PA: Banner of Truth, 1977), pp. 155 and 157.

3. Robert Leighton, quoted in *ibid.*, pp. 156-157.

4. Charles Spurgeon, quoted on the back cover material of Andrew Bonar, ed., *Letters of Samuel Rutherford* (repr., Carlisle, PA: Banner of Truth, 1984).

5. Richard Baxter, *ibid.*

6. *Letters*, pp. 599f., 596.

7. *Ibid.*, pp. 122-123.

8. Andrew Bonar, ed., *Memoir and Remains of Robert Murray M'Cheyne* (repr., Carlisle, PA: Banner of Truth, 1966), pp. 490-495.

9. *Memoir and Remains*, p. 192.

10. *Ibid.*

11. *Ibid.*, p. 496.

12. For Christian heroism on behalf of the Jews during the Holocaust, see the Bibliographical Supplement to this chapter.

13. See Basilea Schlink, *Israel My Chosen People. A German Confession Before God and the Jews* (Old Tappan, NJ: Fleming H. Revell, 1987).

14. Iain Murray, *The Puritan Hope,* p. 154.

15. *Ibid.,* p. 155.

16. H. C. G. Moule, quoted from *The Expositor's Bible* (Vol. V, p. 590), in Steve Schlissel and David Brown, *Hal Lindsey & The Restoration of the Jews* (Edmonton: Still Waters Revival Books, 1990), p. 55. This book consists of a reprint of Brown's 1861 work with a lengthy foreword by Schlissel.

Chapter Four—The Rabbis: Stiff-necked, Hardhearted and Proud?

1. For a very readable study of the life of Rabbi Akiva, see Louis Finkelstein, *Akiva: Scholar, Saint and Martyr* (repr., Northvale, NJ: Jason Aronson, 1990).

2. Jerusalem Talmud, Berakhot 9:7, 14b, translated in C. G. Montefiore and H. Loewe, *Rabbinic Anthology,* pp. 269f. This is probably the oldest Talmudic version of the martyrdom of Rabbi Akiva.

3. This account is quoted in Irving J. Rosenbaum, *The Holocaust and Halakhah,* p. 166, n. 4. I have translated into English some of the Hebrew words found in the original quote.

4. For glowing praises of the Chofetz Chaim, see Rabbi Nosson Scherman in Rabbi Nisson Wolpin, ed., *The Torah Personality. A Treasury of Biographical Sketches* (Brooklyn, NY: Mesorah Publications, 1980), pp. 69-86.

5. Rabbi Zechariah Fendel, *The Halacha and Beyond* (New York: Torah Ethics Library, 1983), p. 121.

6. Quoted from Mendel Weinbach, ed., *Give Us Life. Mesholim* ["Parables"] *and Masterwords of the Chofetz Chaim* (Jerusalem: Shma Yisroel, 1973), p. 174.

7. *Ibid.,* p. 182.

8. *Ibid.,* p. 188.

9. For a discussion of all Talmudic references related to Jesus
   and Messianic Judaism/Christianity, see R. Travis Herford,
   Christianity in Talmud and Midrash (repr., Clifton, NJ: Reference Book Publishers, 1966). A blasphemous work entitled *Toledot Yeshu* ("The History of Jesus"), utilizing some
   of the Talmudic material about Jesus, was composed by
   medieval Jewish writers who, to a great extent, were react-
   ing in anger to the Church's vulgar anti-Semitism. In any
   case, regardless of the reasons for its writing, *Toledot Yeshu*
   bears *no* official status in Judaism, is of *no* historical value
   and has been repudiated by modern Jewish scholars.

10. According to Jacob Neusner, one of the leading authorities
    on early Judaism, rabbinic texts from approximately 70-300
    C.E. represent "Judaism without Christianity," while rab-
    binic texts from roughly 400-600 C.E. represent "Judaism
    despite Christianity." See Jacob Neusner, *The Mishnah. An
    Introduction* (Northvale, NJ: Jason Aronson, 1989), p. 221.

11. See the Bibliographical Supplement to this chapter for a list-
    ing of good introductory studies and anthologies.

12. Mishnah, Pirkei Avot 2:1.

13. Pirkei Avot 1:3.

14. Mishnah, Berakhot 4:4; Babylonian Talmud, Berakhot 31a;
    Berakhot 32b; Ta'anit 2a; Ta'anit 8a. The last four quotes
    are taken from *Words of the Wise. An Anthology of Proverbs
    and Practical Axioms,* compiled by Reuven Alcalay in col-
    laboration with Mordekhai Nurock (Israel: Massada, 1970),
    cols. 381f.

15. Mishnah, Yoma 8:9; Babylonian Talmud, Bava Mesia 58b;
    Berakhot 32a; Yoma 96a; Shabbat 104a. All these quotes are
    taken from *Words of the Wise,* cols. 410f.

16. Moses Maimonides, Hilchot Teshuva ("Laws of Repen-
    tance") 10:3, as translated by Louis Jacobs, *Holy Living.
    Saints and Saintliness in Judaism* (Northvale, NJ: Jason

Aronson, 1990), p. 76. While this and the following quote are not taken directly from the Talmud, they are completely Talmudic in spirit.

17. Sifre Ya'akov, taken from *Words of the Wise*, col. 293.

Chapter Five—Miriam and Jacob: Household Names in the Savior's Home

1. For a very "Jewish" translation of the New Testament, in which all personal and place names are given in their Hebrew or Aramaic forms, see David H. Stern, *Jewish New Testament* (Jerusalem: Jewish New Testament Publications, 1989).

2. This is not a problem in most translations. For example, in German, the Greek name *Iakobos* is properly translated as Jacobus, while in Korean it is Yakov.

3. The name Jeshua occurs in the Old Testament 28 times (one each in First and Second Chronicles, 11 times in Ezra and 15 times in Nehemiah).

4. See again Stern's *Jewish New Testament.*

5. The Hebrew word is *tsitsit,* rendered as *kraspedon* in the Septuagint and in the New Testament (e.g., Matt. 23:5). For the usage and meaning of *kraspedon,* see Walter Bauer, William F. Arndt, F. Wilbur Gingrich and Fredrick W. Danker, *A Greek English Lexicon of the New Testament and Other Early Christian Literature* (Chicago: Univ. of Chicago Press, 1979), p. 448.

6. See the Bibliographical Supplement to this chapter for studies on the Jewishness of Jesus. The verdict of E.P. Sanders, a leading professor at Oxford University, represents the general scholarly consensus: "The synoptic Jesus lived as a law-abiding Jew." See his *Jewish Law from Jesus to the Mishnah. Five Studies* (Philadelphia: Trinity Press Int., 1990), p. 90.

7. For Jesus as King of the Jews, see A. Lukyn Williams, *A Manual of Christian Evidences for Jewish People* (New York: MacMillian and Co., 1911-1919), pp. 29f., sec. 30 (5).

8. For detailed studies on the Epistle of James in its original Jewish context, see James B. Adamson, *James. The Man and His Message* (Grand Rapids: Wm. B. Eerdmans, 1989); Ralph P. Martin, *James,* Word Biblical Commentary (abbreviated hereafter as WBC; Waco, TX: Word, 1988); Peter H. Davids, *Commentary on James,* New International Greek Testament Commentary (Grand Rapids: Wm. B. Eerdmans, 1982).

9. See F. F. Bruce, *The Book of the Acts,* New International Commentary on the New Testament (abbreviated hereafter as NICNT [the Old Testament series is abbreviated as NICOT]; Grand Rapids: Wm. B. Eerdmans, 1988), p. 249, n. 25, where he points out that, "As a Roman citizen, Paul would have had three names...." These names would be in addition to his Hebrew name, *Sha'ul.*

10. See Dan Juster and Keith Intrater, *Israel, the Church and the Last Days* (Shippensburg, PA: Destiny Image, 1990), pp. 267-281. For additional studies on the spiritual and prophetic significance of the biblical holy days, see the Bibliographical Supplement to this chapter.

11. According to the Book of Revelation, the glorified Son of God is "the Lion of the tribe of *Judah,* the Root of *David*" (Rev. 5:5). He is still a Jew! These are His words, spoken in the context of His return: "I am the Root and the Offspring of David, and the bright Morning Star" (Rev. 22:16).

Chapter Six—Bad Reporting, Bias and Bigotry

1. Frank Gervasi, in Stephen Karetzky and Peter Goldman, eds., *The Media's War Against Israel* (New York, Jerusalem, Tel Aviv: Steimatzky-Shapolsky, 1986), p. 263. Not surprisingly, Theodore Winston Pike, *Israel: Our Duty...Our Dilemma* (Oregon City, OR: Big Sky Press, 1984), deals with Israel's involvement in Lebanon in the chapter entitled

"A Forgotten Holocaust" (see pp. 69-73). For an assessment of Pike's book, see below, n. 45.

2. See Fouad Ajami, *Beirut. City of Regrets* (with photographs by Eli Reed; New York: W. W. Norton, 1988), p. 38: "In June [of 1982], the population of South Lebanon had greeted the Israeli army with rice and flowers....Men wanted a return to a normal world, and the invading Israeli army was seen as the best hope of shattering the Palestinian sanctuary, making possible a return to more tranquil times." It should be noted that Prof. Ajami, a recognized Middle East scholar, is by no means biased toward Israel, finding fault with Israel's overall policy in Lebanon.

3. This is amply documented throughout Karetzky and Goldman, *The Media's War;* see also Neil C. Livingstone and David Halevy, *Inside the PLO. Covert Units, Secret Funds, and the War Against Israel and the United States* (New York: William Morrow, 1990); Leonard J. Davis (eds. Eric Rozenmann and Jeff Rubin), *Myths and Facts 1989. A Concise Record of the Israeli-Arab Conflict* (Washington, DC: Near East Reports, 1988), pp. 128-130; and Yitschak Ben Gad, *Politics, Lies and Videotape. 3,000 Questions and Answers on the Mideast Crisis* (New York: Shapolsky Publishers, 1991), pp. 30-54, "PLO Crimes in Lebanon."

4. Frank Gervasi, in *The Media's War,* p. 263.

5. For Hafez Assad of Syria and his atrocities, see Moshe Ma'oz, *Asad. The Sphinx of Damascus. A Political Biography* (New York: Grove Weidenfeld, 1988). The Palestinian terrorist group Black September, responsible for the murder of the Israeli Olympic team in Munich, 1972, was named after these riots; see Livingstone and Halevy, *Inside the PLO,* pp. 103-106.

6. See Davis, *Myths and Facts,* pp. 127f. (dealing with the misconception: "The Palestinians do not have a homeland") and

Ben Gad, *Politics, Lies and Videotape*, pp. 105-118, "Jordan Is Palestine."

7. See Ari and Shira Sorko-Ram, "Who's to Blame for the Temple Mount Riots?", *Maoz Newsletter*, November, 1990, pp. 2f.

8. For an accurate account of the events surrounding the Temple Mount riot, see *ibid.* (entire newsletter).

9. See A. Roy Eckardt, "The Devil and Yom Kippur," reprinted in Talmage, *Disputation and Dialogue*, pp. 232f.

10. Paul Johnson, "Marxism vs. the Jews," *Commentary*, April, 1984, p. 34, quoted in Flannery, *Anguish of the Jews*, pp. 346f., n. 24.

11. See "Israel and the Occupied Territories. Amnesty International's Concerns in 1988" (New York: Amnesty International, 1989). For honest responses to many of the most common charges of Israeli brutality, see Max Singer, "Moral Standards Under Pressure: The Israeli Army and the *Intifada*," *Ethics and International Affairs*, Vol. 4 (1990), pp. 135-143; Davis, *Myths and Facts*, pp. 171-202 ("Israel's Treatment of Minorities/The Uprising"); and "FLAME. Facts and Logic About the Middle East. A sampling of twenty educational and clarifying ads that have been published monthly in major national media" (FLAME: 1991), ad #'s 21a, "Israel and Human Rights. How does Israel behave in the face of Arab uprising?" 26, "The 'Intifada.' Is Israel using excessive force to suppress it?" and 28, "Israel, the Arabs, & Human Rights (1)."

A recent article in *The Jewish Press* (Vol. XLI, No. 29, week of July 19-July 25, 1991, p. 8a) presents "a response to the Amnesty International 1991 annual report from Israel's Ministry of Justice." It notes serious deficiencies in Amnesty's reporting, most notably their failure to provide "background details necessary to evaluate the proportionality of Israel's responses to intifada violence." For example, the 1991 A.I. report omits the fact that "during the relevant year, participants in the intifada perpetrated 71,792 public disturbances, 81 shootings, 5 grenade attacks, 651 molotov cocktail attacks, 94 bombings, 173 'cold' attacks (mostly knives, clubs, axes, and swords), and 299 cases of arson. This violence forced 1193 Israeli civilians and 2815 members of the Israel Defense Forces to secure hospital treament for their injuries." How much of this is reported by the Western Press?

12. See Livingstone and Halevy, *Inside the PLO;* for a concise statement of the UN's bias against Israel, see "FLAME. A sampling," ad # 32, "The U.N. and the Middle East. Is it a proper forum to sit in judgment?"; note also Flannery, *Anguish of the Jews,* p. 346, beginning of n. 24; and the *Jewish Voice Prophetic Magazine,* November, 1991, p. 16 (quoting from the *Jewish Press,* July 26, 1991).

13. See again Livingstone and Halevy, *Inside the PLO.*

14. See Davis, *Myths and Facts,* pp. 27-29; and Rabbi Joseph Telushkin, *Jewish Literacy* (New York: William Morrow and Co., 1991), pp. 277-279 ("Haganah; Irgun—Bombing of the King David Hotel; Lekhi; Palmach"), and pp. 296f. ("Deir Yassin").

15. For just two examples among many, see Davis, *Myths and Facts,* pp. 94f. (dealing with the Israeli government's investigation of the army's alleged complicity in the massacre at the Sabra and Shatilla refugee camps in Lebanon), and pp. 174-176 (dealing with the government's investigation of charges of Israeli torture of Arab prisoners). When the news of the Sabra and Shatilla massacres was made public, 400,000 Israelis gathered in Tel Aviv, calling for a thorough government investigation of the Israeli army's possible involvement in the slaughter. What a display of passion for human rights: Israeli Jews expressing their outrage at the

report that their army might have allowed Arabs to slaughter other Arabs!

16. It is a shocking and horrifying experience to read the Amnesty International reports on torture in countries like Syria, Iraq and Iran; see e.g., "Syria. Torture by the Security Forces," (New York: Amnesty International, 1987), p. 1: "The range of torture methods used is such that it led one former detainee to describe a Damascus detention centre as a 'research centre' for new torture techniques." It is unfair even to compare the practices of these countries with the practices of the Israeli government (see immediately above, nn. 11 and 15).

    Since 1948, law abiding Jews living in Arab countries have at times been harassed, arrested, tortured and even executed (see Davis, *ibid.*, pp. 142-152). In 1969 in Iraq, Jews accused of spying were hung in the public squares of Baghdad. Baghdad Radio "called upon Iraqis to 'come and enjoy the feast.' Some 500,000 men, women and children paraded and danced past the scaffolds where the bodies of the hanged Jews swung; the mob rhythmically chanted 'Death to Israel' and 'Death to all traitors.' " (Davis, *ibid.*, p. 147). Yet Israel has never even executed a single Arab *terrorist,* regardless of the crimes committed. (Adolf Eichmann, the notorious Nazi criminal, was the only person executed in Israel's modern history.)

17. Gervasi, in *The Media's War,* pp. 242-245.

18. See Singer, "Moral Standards," p. 137, n. 3.

19. See "The PLO. Has It Complied With Its Commitments?", with an update, August 1990 (Jerusalem: Ministry of Foreign Affairs, 1990), p. 3.

20. Interview with *Politiken,* Denmark, cited in *ibid.,* p. 8. Kadoumi is known within the PLO as Abu Lutf ("Father of Kindness").

21. The recent war to liberate Kuwait provided an excellent example of this: Israel was commended because it refused to retaliate against Saddam Hussein. What other nation would be asked to sit back and be bombed repeatedly, allowing its people to be terrorized and its properties devastated for the sake of an international coalition?

22. "The Devil and Yom Kippur," p. 232.

23. Stokely Carmichael, (now Kwame Toure), quoted in Prager and Telushkin, *Why the Jews?*, p. 149.

24. Cited in the ADL Research Report, "Louis Farrakhan: The Campaign to Manipulate Public Opinion" (New York: Anti-Defamation League of B'nai B'rith, 1990), pp. 41 and 43.

25. *Ibid.*, pp. 31f.

26. *Ibid.*, pp. 49 and 47. Of course, Farrakhan does not speak for all Black Americans. The most influential Black leader of this century, Martin Luther King, was a real friend of the Jews. For representative quotes, see Gould, *What Did They Think of the Jews?*, pp. 566-569. Note p. 568: "wherever we have seen anti-Semitism we have condemned it with all our might."

27. David Duke, quoted by Rabbi Marvin Hier, letter from the Simon Wiesenthal Center (1990), p. 2.

28. See John W. Whitehead, "The fatal consequences of hatred," *Action* (A Monthly Publication of The Rutherford Institute), June 1991, pp. 3f.; and James Ridgeway, *Blood in the Face: The Ku Klux Klan, Aryan Nations, Nazi Skinheads, and the Rise of the New White Culture* (New York: Thunder's Mouth Press, 1991).

29. Cited in the ADL Research Report "Liberty Lobby: Network of Hate" (New York: Anti-Defamation League of B'nai B'rith, 1990), p. 5.

30. Martin Luther, quoted in Lucy S. Dawidowicz, *The War Against the Jews 1933-1945* (New York: Bantam, 1986), p. 23. It is painful to read Luther's words: "Verily a hopeless, wicked, venomous and devilish thing is the existence of these Jews, who for fourteen hundred years have been, and still are, our pest, torment and misfortune. They are just devils and nothing more" (quoted in Hay, *Christian Anti-Semitism*, p. 167). The sentiments against the Jews expressed by Erasmus, the Christian humanist and theological opponent of Luther, are not much better: "Who is there among us who does not hate this race of men?...If it is Christian to hate the Jews, here we are all Christians in profusion" (quoted in Jonathan I. Israel, *European Jewry in the Age of Mercantilism* [Oxford: Oxford Univ. Press, 1985], p. 15; and see Paul Johnson, *A History of the Jews* [New York: Harper & Row, 1987], p. 241).

31. "Liberty Lobby," p. 10.

32. *Ibid.,* p. 2, my italics.

33. *The Nationalist,* pp. 3f.

34. Prager and Telushkin, *Why the Jews?* p. 124. For further shocking quotes, see Davis, *Myths and Facts,* pp. 273-282.

35. Robert Lacey, *The Kingdom* (New York: Harcourt Brace Jovanovich, 1981), p. 259.

36. *Ibid.,* pp. 385f.

37. Quoted in Ben Gad, *Politics, Lies and Videotape,* p. 250. Ben Gad's entire book is filled with similar quotes from Arab spokesmen.

38. Quoted in George Grant, *The Blood of the Moon* (Brentwood, TN: Wolgemuth & Hyatt, 1991), p. 53. See p. 122, n. 4, for the source. Grant supplies other quotes from past and present Arab leaders, all calling for the murder of all Jews in Israel. See pp. 53-56. Note the words of Syria's Hafez Assad: "We have resolved to drench this land with

Israel's blood, to oust the Jews as aggressors, and to throw them into the sea" (p. 56).

39. Quoted in Ben Gad, p. 181. Hussein's declaration of June 8, 1967, spoken on Amman Radio, was preceded by this June 7 broadcast on Damascus Radio: "Soldiers of the fronts of Jordan, Syria, Gaza, and Khan Yunis—the holy march is on! Kill them and cleanse their blood off your weapons on the shores of Jaffa, Acco, and Haifa." (Quoted in *ibid.*)

40. Louis A. DeCaro, *Israel Today: Fulfillment of Prophecy?* (Presbyterian and Reformed Pub. Co.: 1974), p. 22. DeCaro's book was praised by respected authors such as Johannes G. Vos ("I am impressed with its high degree of Biblical scholarship, good sense, and sound point of view.") and Loraine Boettner ("More effectively than any other writer that I have read, he maintains that the State of Israel...has no basis whatever in Biblical prophecy, and that it is based on the same political and military principles that activate the other nations of the world.") Both are quoted on the back cover, and Professor Vos provided the Foreword.

41. See the relevant sections of Davis, *Myths and Facts.*

42. Pike, *Israel: Our Duty...Our Dilemma*, p. 283.

43. Rick Godwin, from his 1988 audio tape series "The Shepherd-Sheep Relationship."

44. Ray Sutton, "Does Israel Have a Future?", *Covenant Renewal Newsletter,* Vol. 11, No. 12 (December, 1988), p. 3 (distributed by the Institute for Christian Economics, Tyler, TX). Ray Sutton, formerly a pastor in Texas, is now the president of the Philadelphia Theological Seminary.

45. Pike, *Israel,* p. 280. Pike's book serves as a classic example of militantly anti-Jewish writing. From a historical standpoint, it is filled with gross errors and inaccuracies; even the spelling of cited Jewish sources is often totally confused. In

terms of Pike's evaluation of Jewish history, Judaism and the modern state of Israel (called "the Mother of Harlots" on p. 279), the book is devoid of scholarly value. In light of this, the back cover blurb is almost unbelievable: "A spellbinding thesis. Unprecedented. The most specific, accurate, and comprehensive overview of Jewish history and aspirations available today."

According to Pike, who by his own definition would *not* qualify as an anti-Semite (see p. 329), Jewish aspirations are definite and clear: "Both the Talmud and the Kabbalah predestine the Church in America to the same fate as was meted out during the last 67 years to well over 100 million 'goyim' ['Gentiles'] in nearly one-third of the world: death by starvation, slaughter, torture, imprisonment and exhaustion. Do not think that there is the tiniest particle of gratitude within the Zionist for the charity and money and munitions which Christians have invested in the Israeli experiment....*All the Church will ever receive from Zionism for her kindness is what Gus Hall promised Christianity in America: a bullet in the belly.* Instead of being 'blessed' in return for our 'blessing' of the Jews, we can only anticipate from Zionism generations of slavery in the worldwide Gulag [prison system] to come" (p. 293, Pike's emphasis).

Pike's words would be applauded and affirmed by anti-Semites like the late King Faisal of Saudi Arabia or the "moderate" Egyptian author Anis Mansur. Faisal claimed that "Zionists...are there to destroy all human organizations and to destroy civilization and the work which good people are trying to do." Mansur, in his book *Wound in the Heart of Israel,* said, "The world must curse the Jews, and curse the day on which they came on earth...The Jews prepare for humanity every form of torture..." (Both are quoted in Ben Gad, *Politics, Lies and Videotape,* pp. 250 and 433.) How awful that "Christian" and Muslim can unite in villifying the Jews!

Chapter Seven—Lies! Lies! Lies!

1. See Yvonne Glikson, "Wandering Jew," *Encyclopedia Judaica*, Vol. 16 (Jerusalem: Keter, 1971), cols. 259-263.

2. For anti-Semitism and the Black Death, see Flannery, *Anguish of the Jews*, pp. 109-111.

3. Haim Hillel Ben-Sasson, *Trial and Achievement: Currents in Jewish History*, pp. 254-255, quoted in Prager and Telushkin, *Why the Jews?*, p. 102.

4. Prager and Telushkin, *ibid.*, p. 103. See also Cecil Roth, "Host, Desecration of," *Enc. Jud.*, Vol. 8, cols. 1040-1044.

5. See R. Po-chia Hsia, *The Myth of Ritual Murder. Jews and Magic in Reformation Germany* (New Haven: Yale Univ. Press, 1988); Trachtenberg, *The Devil and the Jews*, pp. 97-155; and Haim Hillel Ben-Sasson and Yehuda Slutsky, "Blood Libel," *Enc. Jud.*, Vol. 4, cols. 1120-1131, with the literature cited there (especially the works of H. L. Strack and Cecil Roth).

6. Simon Wiesenthal, *Every Day Remembrance Day, A Chronicle of Jewish Martyrdom* (New York: Henry Holt and Co., 1987), p. 100.

7. See Flannery, *ibid.*, pp. 16f.

8. It was printed in 1973 and found by Prager and Telushkin; see *Why the Jews?*, p. 99.

9. The booklet, entitled *Jewish Ritual Murder*, was written by Arnold Leese; see Flannery, *ibid.*, p. 318, n. 53.

10. James Parkes, *The Foundations of Judaism and Christianity*, quoted in Prager and Telushkin, *ibid.*, p. 100.

11. Prager and Telushkin, *ibid.*, pp. 100f.

12. Hier, Wiesenthal Center letter, p. 3 (my italics). For the history of the Damascus Blood Libel, see H. H. Ben-Sasson,

ed., *A History of the Jewish People* (Eng. trans., Cambridge, MA: Harvard Univ. Press, 1976), pp. 847-849.

13. See World Jewish Congress, *News & Views,* Vol. XV, No. 3 (Feb.-April 1991), p. 20.

14. Here are typical quotes: "The truth is that not one single Jew was killed in the gas chambers, and the latter were simply used for disinfection of the inmate's clothes. The gas could not kill people anyway, and the chambers could have never handled the amounts of people that Israel is talking about. The international community must stop Israel and hold her responsible for all her crimes so as not to allow her to grow into as destructive an entity as Naziism." (*Sawt-al-Arab* ["Arab Voice"], Cairo, July 14, 1986; quoted in Davis, *Myths and Facts,* p. 281); "...the holocaust is primarily an historical hoax...the greatest holocaust was not against Jews, but perpetrated on Christians by Jews.... I question whether 6 million Jews actually died in Nazi death camps" ("David Duke: In His Own Words. A Sampler of bigotry, racism and anti-Semitism" [New York: Anti-Defamation League of B'nai B'rith, n.d.], p. 3). For further bibliography, with reference to Arthur R. Butz' infamous work, *The Hoax of the Twentieth Century,* see the Bibliographical Supplement to this chapter.

15. "Even if we accept the Jewish figures of six million Jewish martyrs in the Holocaust (a figure many scholars believe to be the wildest exaggeration), still that figure shrivels before the estimated 144 million victims of Jewish-inspired communism since 1917" (Pike, *Israel,* p. 174).

16. Cited in Hier, Wiesenthal Center letter, pp. 2f.

17. Anyone who has ever read a book like Martin Gilbert's *The Holocaust* or viewed photographs like those collected in Yitzhak Arad's *Pictorial History of the Holocaust,* let alone visited the Yad Vashem museum in Jerusalem, can only wish

that the Holocaust never happened. It is almost impossible to comprehend that these things took place in "civilized" Europe one generation ago. See the Bibliographical Supplement to Chapter One for a listing of several key Holocaust works.

18. With the recent rise of *glasnost* ("openness") in Russia, Jews are now being accused, quite openly, of being the cause of that nation's economic chaos and near collapse.

19. Hier, Wiesenthal Center letter, p. 3. For a study of international financial pressure exerted *against* Israel by the Arab world, see Aaron J. Sarna, *Boycott and Blacklist. A History of Arab Economic Warfare Against Israel* (Totowa, NJ: Rowman & Littlefield, 1986).

20. See, e.g., Pike, *Israel,* pp. 141-164 ("Soviet Anti- Semitism: 'Red' Herring?") and pp. 166-177 ("Monopolists of the Media"); see also *ibid.,* p. 174, quoted immediately above, n. 15. When King Faisal of Saudi Arabia was asked how he could reconcile his claim that "Zionism is the mother of Communism" with "the fact that Israel and the USSR appeared to be on opposite sides in the Middle East, with the Russians providing weapons for Egypt and Syria to use against the Jews," he confidently answered: "It's all part of a great plot, a grand conspiracy. Communism...is a Zionist creation designed to fulfill the aims of Zionism. They are only pretending to work against each other" (Robert Lacey, *The Kingdom,* p. 386).

In her Foreword to the reprint of Hay's *Christian Anti-Semitism,* p. xi, Claire Hutchet Bishop wrote: "Accused yesterday of being communists and accused today of being capitalists, Jews have no right to exist as Jews." Also relevant is the comment of George Orwell: "Obviously, the charges against the Jews are not true. They cannot be true, partly because they cancel out, partly because no one people could have such a monopoly of wickedness" (quoted in Gould, *What Did They Think of the Jews?*, p. 471).

21. Micah H. Naftalin, National Director of the Union of Councils for Soviet Jews, letter (1990), p. 1: "An official magazine of the Soviet Defense Ministry began to serialize [these] two works deemed to be 'must' reading for the rising officers of the Red Army." For more on the *Protocols,* see the Bibliographical Supplement to this chapter.

22. Cf. Pike, *Israel,* p. 328: "The truth is, the majority of Jews living in Palestine high-handedly expelling Arabs from their homes are no more the descendants of Abraham than such Jewish converts as Sammy Davis, Jr., Marilyn Monroe, or for that matter, the rest of us." Cf. also Charles D. Provan, *The Church Is Israel Now. The Transfer of Conditional Privilege* (Vallectio, CA: Ross House Books, 1987), p. 29: "...Jews trace their lineage [through Isaac] (a fact which is greatly open to dispute)."

Concerning the myth that the original Jews were all black, cf. the words of Kwame Toure (formerly Stokely Carmichael): "Africa gave Judaism to the world. Moses was an Egyptian! Moses was an African!" (quoted in Gould, *What Did They Think of the Jews?*, p. 570). As for the Black Hebrew cult (this has nothing to do with Ethiopian Jews, who *should* be accepted as Jews), see Davis, *Myths and Facts,* pp. 18-20. For an accurate statement on the diversity of races represented among the Jewish people, see Flannery, *Anguish of the Jews,* p. 331, n. 5.

23. The standard work on this subject is Arthur Koestler, *The Thirteenth Tribe. The Khazar Empire and Its Heritage* (New York: Random House, 1976). Its conclusions are accepted as virtual fact by Pike, *Israel,* pp. 326-328 and James McKeever, *Claim Your Birthright* (Medford, OR: Omega Publications), pp. 173ff. (McKeever is an internationally respected economist, as well as a best-selling Christian

author. *Claim Your Birthright* received "the prestigious Angel Award" for fine Christian writing.) For the scholarly refutation of Koestler's claims, see the Bibliographical Supplement to this chapter.

24. See John Powledge, *Replacement Theology: The Denial of Covenant?* (M. Div. thesis, Messiah Biblical Institute and Graduate School of Theology: 1991), Appendix C: "McKeever, Koestler and the Khazars: Questions of Validity and Factuality in Historical Research."

25. In the eyes of the traditional Jewish community, one of the greatest problems facing American Jewry today is *assimilation* through intermarriage with Gentiles. See Telushkin, *Jewish Literacy,* pp. 441-444 ("The Vanishing American Jew. Low Birthrate, Assimilation, and Intermarriage").

26. Louis Farrakhan, quoted in Gould, *What Did They Think of the Jews?,* pp. 559f. (beginning at the bottom of p. 559).

27. Richard Wagner, quoted in *ibid.,* p. 192.

28. These—and a host of other charges—are tragically brought by Pike, *Israel,* pp. 20-105 and 296-324, and then repeated by McKeever, pp. 265-279; cf. also Gary North, *The Judeo-Christian Tradition: A Guide for the Perplexed* (Tyler, TX: Institute for Christian Economics, 1990), pp. 73-130. It is really a terrible shame that many Christians will read these Talmudic passages, taken out of context and woefully misinterpreted by Pike, McKeever and to a lesser extent, North, and draw a perverted picture of traditional Judaism (and traditional Jews!). The comment of Moses Mielziner still holds true: "It is certain that many of those who...pass a condemning judgment upon the gigantic work of the Talmud never read nor were able to read a single page of the same in the original, but were prompted by religious prejudice and antagonism, or they based their verdict merely on those disconnected and often distorted passages which

Eisenmenger and his consorts and followers picked out from the Talmud for hostile purposes" (*Introduction to the Talmud. With a new bibliography, 1925-1967 by Alexander Guttmann* [New York: Bloch Pub. Co., 1968], p. 103). For literature on the attacks against the Talmud, beginning with the notorious work of J. A. Eisenmenger, see the Bibliographical Supplement to this chapter.

29. See Prager and Telushkin, *Why the Jews?*, pp. 46-58.

30. This incredibly twisted lie can be found both in Pike's book, *Israel: Our Duty...Our Dilemma*, p. 36, n. 6, as well as in his companion video, "The Other Israel."

31. These misconceptions are dealt with throughout Davis, *Myths and Facts*.

32. Michael Comay, *Zionism, Israel, and the Palestinian Arabs. Questions and Answers* (Jerusalem: Keter, 1983), p. 40. See also Ben Gad, *Politics, Lies and Videotape*, pp. 155f., "Israel: Never an Arab Land."

33. See Davis, *ibid.*, pp. 21-29.

34. See Comay, *ibid.*, pp. 40-44, and Davis, *ibid.*, pp. 24-73, 85. Note also Davis, *ibid.*, p. 128: "From 1965 until the 1982 Israeli operation in Lebanon, 689 Israelis lost their lives and 3799 were wounded in PLO terrorist attacks."

35. David A. Rausch, *A Legacy of Hatred: Why Christians Must Not Forget the Holocaust* (Grand Rapids: Baker, 1990), p. 183. While the Arab nations were urging the Palestinians to temporarily abandon the Land, resident Jews were urging them to stay! Ben Gad, *Politics, Lies and Videotape*, pp. 306f., gives the complete text of a poster of the Haifa (Jewish) Workers Council from April 28, 1948, "appealing to Arabs to remain in their homes and jobs." Palestinian Arabs who did not flee the Land were granted full citizenship.

36. See conveniently, "Whatever the Names the Aim Is the Same" (Israel Information Centre, n.d.); and Davis, *Myths and Facts*, pp. 283-294 (esp. pp. 291ff.).

37. See Davis, *Myths and Facts*, pp. 12f. (with a graphic quote from Mark Twain describing Palestine in 1867).

38. See Ben Gad, *Politics, Lies and Videotape*, pp. 311ff. and 138.

39. Ralph Galloway, quoted in Ari and Shira Sorko-Ram, "A Short Handbook on the Israeli-Arab Conflict. The Palestinian Problem," *Maoz Newsletter*, p. 4. See the graphic truths presented by Ben Gad, *ibid.*, pp. 291-308, "Palestinian Arab Refugees—Political Weapons in Cruel Arab Hands."

40. Hanifi Younes, quoted in *USA Today*, International Edition, March 8, 1991, section A, p. 2. Regarding Yassir Arafat, Younes says: "I hate that man. Every time he opens his mouth, he causes us trouble. I have nothing to do with him. Why do I have to be held responsible for what he says?" Similar quotes from other Palestinians are readily available.

41. See "Judea Samaria and the Gaza District since 1967" (Jerusalem: Israel Information Centre, 1986); and Davis, *Myths and Facts*, pp. 178f., 181-189.

42. See *ibid.*, pp. 74f., and "FLAME. A sampling," introductory letter (inside cover) and ad # 25 (" 'Land for Peace.' Can it solve the problems of the Middle East?").

43. Ben Gad, *Politics, Lies and Videotape*, p. 262.

44. Quoted in *ibid.*

45. Quoted in *ibid.*

46. See the ADL Report on Louis Farrakhan, pp. 11-13. Steve Cokely was an aide to Mayor Eugene Sawyer;

Sawyer dismissed him in 1988 when Cokely's virulent anti-Semitism came to light.

47. For all these lies, see Clifford Goldstein, "The Patagonian Zionist Plot," *Shabbat Shalom*, July-September 1990, pp. 12-14.

48. See Hier, Wiesenthal Center letter, p. 1.

Chapter Eight—The Inquisition Isn't Over

1. See Cecil Roth, *A History of the Marranos* (New York: Schocken, 1974); Yitzhak Baer, *A History of the Jews in Christian Spain*, Vol. 2 (trans. by Louis Schoffman; Philadelphia: Jewish Publication Society, 1966). Note the comment of Major Arthur Griffiths: "The fires of the modern Inquisition, it was said, had been lighted exclusively for the Jews" (*In Spanish Prisons. The Inquisition at Home and Abroad. Prisons Past and Present* [repr., New York: Dorset Press, 1991], p. 32).

2. Rafael Sabatini, *Torquemada—The Spanish Inquisition* (Boston/New York: Houghton-Mifflin Pub., 1924), pp. 265f.

3. *Ibid.*, pp. 266-268.

4. These were the ordinances laid down by St. Dominic: "The penitent...must not eat any kind of meat during his whole life;...must wear a religious dress with a small cross embroidered on each breast; must attend mass every day, if he has the means of doing so, and vespers on Sunday and festivals; must recite the service for the day and night and repeat the paternoster ["Our Father"] seven times in the day, ten times in the evening, and twenty times at midnight. If he failed in any of these requirements, he was to be burned as a 'relapsed heretic' " (Griffiths, *ibid.*, pp. 16f.).

5. Quoted in Ben-Sasson, *A History of the Jewish People*, p. 589.

6. Charlotte Klein, *Anti-Judaism in Christian Theology,* p. 11.

7. For in-depth studies of these verses, see W. D. Davies and Dale C. Allison, *The Gospel According to Saint Matthew,* International Critical Commentary (abbreviated hereafter as ICC; Edinburgh: T & T Clark, 1988), Vol. 1, pp. 481-503; Robert A. Guelich, *The Sermon on the Mount* (Waco, TX: Word, 1982), pp. 134-174; and Gustaf Dalman, *Jesus-Jeshua. Studies in the Gospels* (trans. by Paul P. Levertoff; repr., New York: Ktav, 1971), pp. 56-85.

8. Jules Isaac, *Genèse de l'Antisémitisme,* p. 147, quoted in Jaques Doukhan, *Drinking at the Sources. An Appeal to the Jew and the Christian to note their common beginnings,* (trans. by Walter R. Beach and Robert M. Johnson; Mountain View, CA: Pacific Press, 1981), p. 25. Isaac's statement is primarily applicable to Jewish-Christian schisms *after* the first century of this era. See also James Parkes, *The Conflict of the Church and the Synagogue. A Study in the Origins of Antisemitism* (New York: Atheneum, 1985), p. 45.

9. Under the terms of the New Covenant, all of us now "have confidence to enter the Most Holy Place by the blood of Jesus...having our hearts sprinkled to cleanse us from a guilty conscience and having our bodies washed with pure water" (Heb. 10:19, 22). In Jesus the Messiah, Jew and Gentile "are being built together to become a dwelling in which God lives by His Spirit" (Eph. 2:22); in fact, we are *now* seated with Jesus in the heavenly realms (Eph. 2:6), and "every spiritual blessing" in the heavenlies is ours through Him (Eph. 1:3). As we "with unveiled faces all reflect the Lord's glory, [we] are being transformed into His likeness with ever-increasing glory, which comes from the Lord, who is the Spirit" (2 Cor. 3:18). The New Covenant is inexpressibly glorious!

10. See the Bibliographical Supplement to this chapter for more on the question of Sabbath observance.

11. Similar accusations are all too common, as reflected in the following (typical) quote: "The Church of the New Testament was a Jewish sect (Acts 28:22) and dominated by Spirit-filled teachers who had been raised in Judaism. They brought the things of the Old Covenant into the Church, and these things are a snare and a deception which prevent any possibility of corporate Christian maturity.

"The Church at Jerusalem was so infantile that they continued to KEEP THE LAW OF MOSES....As long as we are deceived into copying the pattern of the New Testament Church, we will be bound by satan, just as our long-deceased brethren, the Jerusalem Jews, were bound" (Peter Whyte, *The King and His Kingdom* [Shippensburg, PA: Destiny Image, 1989], p. 89). While Whyte makes some fine points in his book, it is unfortunate that he classifies many of today's problems in the Church under the heading of *Judaistic Christianity,* stating clearly that, "Any 'church' that continues to promote and practice Judaistic Christianity is practicing 'sweet rebellion' against the King, albeit in His Name" (p. 93).

For a brief discussion of the major objections to Jewish believers living as Jews, see David H. Stern, *Messianic Jewish Manifesto* (Jerusalem: Jewish New Testament Publications, 1988), pp. 11-16.

12. For a convenient summary, see Daniel C. Juster, *Jewishness and Jesus* (Downers Grove, IL: InterVarsity Press, 1977), pp. 8ff.

13. There is absolutely no scriptural evidence that Paul yielded to external Judaizing pressure here and compromised his convictions. That would mean that he gave place to something akin to the Galatian heresy, *another gospel.* In other words (actually in Paul's own words), he would have been worthy of *eternal condemnation* (see Galatians 1:6-9). Throughout the rest of the Book of Acts, Paul never once

repudiated his actions in the Temple in Acts 21; rather he pointed to them as praiseworthy (e.g., Acts 24:17ff.; 25:8). And if Paul was not living as a Torah observant Jew, why did he take a Nazarene vow earlier in Acts (Acts 18:18)? Who was he trying to impress then, or what Judaizers were trying to pressure him? The only honest answer is that he did what he did because he himself was "living in obedience to the law" (Acts 21:24). As W. L. Knox wrote regarding Paul, "Obedience to the Law was a life-long matter." See his *St. Paul and the Church of Jerusalem*, p. 122, n. 54, quoted in W. D. Davies, *Paul and Rabbinic Judaism. Some Rabbinic Elements in Pauline Theology* (Philadelphia: Fortress Press, 1980), p. 70, n. 2.

14. See C. Thomas Rhyne, *Faith Establishes the Law* (Chico, CA: Scholars Press, 1981), for a detailed study of this verse.

15. See the Bibliographical Supplement to this chapter, as well as the one to Chapter Five.

16. Note the comment of Knox, *ibid.*, quoted in Davies, *ibid.*, p. 70, n. 3; for a full treatment of these verses from a somewhat different perspective, see Gordon D. Fee, *The First Epistle to the Corinthians*, NICNT (Grand Rapids: Wm. B. Eerdmans, 1987), pp. 422-433.

Chapter Nine—Are You a Crusader for Christ?

1. Benjamin Shlomo Hamburger, *False Messiahs and Their Opposers* (Hebrew; B'nai Brak, Israel: Mechon Moreshet Ashkenaz, 1989), p. 19 (the quotation at the end of the paragraph is from Rav Shimon Walbah, a leading Orthodox rabbi in Israel).

2. Rabbi Ephraim Oshry, *Responsa from the Holocaust,* (Eng. trans., New York: Judaica Press, 1989), pp. xix-xx.

3. *Ibid.,* p. xxi.

4. Eugene B. Borowitz, *Liberal Judaism* (New York: Union of American Hebrew Congregations, 1984), pp. 78f., and 81. Professor Jacob Neusner makes reference to that "religion of love that Christians hear themselves preach (but Jews find scarce in practice)." See his article, "The Myth of the Racism of Judaism," *Judaica Book News,* Vol. 21, Num. 2 (Spring/Summer 1991/5751), p. 27.

5. Eliezer Berkovits, "Judaism in the Post-Christian Era," reprinted in Talmage, *Disputation and Dialogue,* p. 287.

6. *Ibid.,* pp. 287f.

7. Franz Delitzsch, quoted in Schlissel and Brown, *Hal Lindsey & The Restoration of the Jews,* p. 46, n. 57.

8. Nicolai Berdyaev, quoted in Doukhan, *Drinking at the Sources,* p. 93. Note also the words of Basilea Schlink, addressed primarily to her fellow German Christians: "How are the Jews to believe in Jesus? Have we not ourselves blindfolded them? They cannot see Jesus because of our conduct. They cannot believe in Him, because in our lives we have not presented to them the image of Jesus; rather we have shown them the image of mercilessness" (*Israel, My Chosen People. A German Confession Before God and the Jews* [Old Tappan, NJ: Fleming H. Revell, 1987], p. 36).

9. For literature on the Crusades, see the Bibliographical Supplement to this chapter, and note also above, Chapter Two, n. 9.

10. David Rausch, *Legacy of Hatred,* p. 27, provides a vivid account: "They burned the Jews alive in the chief synagogue [of Jerusalem], circling the screaming, flame-tortured humanity singing 'Christ We Adore Thee!' with their Crusader crosses held high." As described by Robert Payne, "The massacre at Jerusalem was carried out deliberately; it was the result of settled policy. Jerusalem was to become a Christian city. The Jews, too, must be destroyed. They had

all rushed to the chief synagogue, where they hoped to receive shelter and protection. The Crusaders, hungry for simple solutions, burned down the synagogue with the Jews inside" (*The Dream and the Tomb. A History of the Crusades* [New York: Dorset Press, 1984], pp. 102f.). Earlier that day, while the Crusaders "ran over the mutilated bodies [of those they had killed] as though they were a carpet spread for them," one of their leaders, Raymond of Aguilers, quoted Psalm 118:22 with approval: "This is the day the Lord has made. We shall rejoice and be glad in it" (*ibid.*, p. 102).

11. Simon R. Schwarzfuchs, "The Crusades," *Enc. Jud.*, Vol. 5, cols. 1137f.

12. *Ibid.*, cols. 1138f.

13. *Ibid.*, col. 1140.

14. Oshry, *Responsa*, p. 64.

15. James Parkes, *The Conflict of the Church and the Synagogue*, p. 395.

16. *Ibid.*, p. 394.

17. *Ibid.*, p. 398.

18. *Ibid.*, p. 399.

19. *Ibid.*, p. 397.

20. *Ibid.*, p. 397.

Chapter Ten—"More Tears"

1. Bonar, *Memoir and Remains of Robert Murray M'Cheyne*, p. 192.

2. Prager and Telushkin, *Why the Jews?*, pp. 17f.

3. See Gary D. Eisenberg, *Smashing the Idols. A Jewish Inquiry into the Cult Phenomenon* (Northvale, NJ: Jason Aronson, 1988).

4. For the classic account of the terrible destruction of Jerusalem just forty years later, see Galya Cornfeld, ed., *Josephus. The Josephus War* (Grand Rapids: Zondervan, 1982).

5. See Michael L. Brown, *How Saved Are We?* (Shippensburg, PA: Destiny Image, 1990), "The Baptism of Tears," pp. 77-84, with relevant quotes from Richard Wurmbrand, John G. Lake, Smith Wigglesworth and others.

6. Wiesenthal, *Every Day Remembrance Day,* pp. 135-137.

Chapter Eleven—So Near and Yet So Far

1. Rabbi Moses Isserles (16th century, Poland), as edited by Rabbi Jacob Berman, *Popular Halacha,* I (Eng. trans., Jerusalem: The World Zionist Organization, 1978), p. 1. These words come from Rabbi Isserles' opening comments to Rabbi Joseph Karo's *Shulchan Arukh* ("Prepared Table").

2. Babyloninan Talmud, Berakhot 63a.

3. Fendel, *The Halachah and Beyond,* p. 18.

4. Unless otherwise noted, the English translation of the prayers cited is from Rabbi Nosson Scherman, ed. and trans., *The Complete Artscroll Siddur* (Brooklyn: Mesorah Pub., 1987); I have substituted "the Lord" for "HaShem" (literally, "the Name"; see p. xvii). For the prayer upon rising in the morning, see pp. 2f. For studies on Jewish prayer in general, see the Bibliographical Supplement to this chapter.

5. *Ibid.*

6. See Dr. Joseph H. Hertz, ed., *The Authorized Daily Prayer Book* (rev. ed.; New York: Bloch Pub. Co., 1971), p. 997, bottom; cf. *Artscroll Siddur,* pp. 288f.

7. Eliezer Berkovits, *With God in Hell,* pp. 17f.

8. See the Hertz *Prayer Book,* pp. 6-9, where the translation of Israel Zangwill is used; cf. *Artscroll Siddur,* pp. 12f.

9. Hertz, *ibid.,* p. 8, bottom.

10. *Artscroll Siddur,* pp. 52-55.

11. Yossel Rakover was a member of a Hasidic (Ultra-Orthodox) family that was wiped out by the Nazis. Although he left behind no written testimony, the words of this moving confession were put into his mouth by Zvi Kolitz, answering the question: "How would a Jew address himself to God at this time?" See Zvi Kolitz, "Yossel Rakover's Appeal to God," in Albert H. Friedlander, ed., *Out of the Whirlwind: A Reader of Holocaust Literature* (New York: Schocken; 1976), pp. 390-399; see also Emil L. Fackenheim, "The People Israel Lives," reprinted in Talmage, *Disputation and Dialogue,* pp. 302f. The prayerful poem entitled, "The Resurrection," quoted by Fackenheim, *ibid.,* pp. 300-302, is another deeply disturbing, text.

12. Cf. *Artscroll Siddur,* pp. 180f.

13. All the following prayers are taken from the *Shemoneh Esrei,* the Eighteen Benedictions, also called the *Amidah* ("The Standing [Prayer]"), or simply, *Tefillah,* "The Prayer" (because it is the Jewish prayer *par excellence*).

Chapter Twelve—Has God Forsaken His People?

1. Remarkably enough, this is basically the conclusion that Charles Provan draws (*The Church Is Israel Now,* pp. 44 and 60-61). In fact, on p. 60 he quotes Jeremiah 31:31-35, but 31:36-37 is *not* quoted. This makes a great difference! (It is contextually impossible also: Jeremiah 31:35 *introduces* verses 36-37; it does not *conclude* verses 31-34.)

2. Commenting on Isaiah 66:22—" 'As the new heavens and the new earth that I make will endure before Me,' declares the LORD, 'so will your name and descendants endure' "—Franz Delitzsch says, "...the seed and name of Israel, i.e.

Israel as a people with the same ancestors and an independent name, continues for ever, like the new heaven and the new earth." See Delitzsch in C. F. Keil and F. Delitzsch, *Commentary on the Old Testament, Isaiah* (trans. by James Martin; repr., Grand Rapids: Wm. B. Eerdmans, 1973), Vol. 7, Part Two, p. 515.

According to James McKeever, however, those who believe "there must be some special place that God has for the nation of Israel," do so *"out of their human emotions....They have absolutely no biblical basis for this belief, only what they have been fed propaganda-wise all of their lives"* (*The End Newsletter*, October, 1989, p. 11, my emphasis); and Charles Provan has written that those who believe the Jews are God's chosen people show *"the sorry state of affairs which exists when the Bible is not studied..."* (*Ibid.*, p. 34, my emphasis). Does this mean that Delitzsch, one of the most spiritually penetrating biblical scholars of the nineteenth century, did not study the Bible?

3. According to Robert Carroll, a noted scholar on the book of Jeremiah, the deep feelings expressed by the words, "My heart yearns for him" describe "the physically powerful urges a mother feels for a son or lovers for each other." That is how God feels for Israel, even in times of disobedience! See Robert P. Carroll, *Jeremiah: A Commentary*, Old Testament Library (Philadelphia: Westminster, 1986), pp. 596f. Carroll further adds: "The images of overwhelming feminine love for her son characterize the deity's view of the community and bespeak a glowing future for it.... Yahweh's love for Ephraim is so strong, so visceral, that the child will encounter mercy in spite of his foolish youthfulness" (p. 600).

4. Nowhere is this view seen more clearly than in the myth of the Wandering Jew. See above, Chapter Seven, "Lies! Lies! Lies!"

5. According to David Chilton, "Because Israel committed the supreme act of covenant breaking when she rejected Christ, Israel herself was rejected by God…" (*Paradise Restored. A Biblical Theology of Dominion* [Tyler, TX: Reconstruction Press, 1985], p. 82); and DeCaro concludes that, "Israel after the flesh, that is, Israel today that believes not in Jesus, may have the right to a political and national distinction…but that distinction remains unrelated to prophetic and covenant redemption" (*Israel Today*, p. 123). Godwin is even more clear: "None of our [spiritual] founding fathers ever believed in a national restoration of a nation of Israel on the earth during any millenium, or that the Jewish nation after the flesh would ever be a select, special people" (audio tape message, "The One Fold of God," from the series "The Shepherd-Sheep Relationship"). It should be noted that Chilton does have a somewhat positive view of the future of *individual Jews* according to Romans 11:26.

6. Godwin again is especially strong on this point: "Not one apostle, not one New Testament writer promises them any restoration of dirt land anywhere in the New Testament" (from his "Shepherd-Sheep" tape series).

7. For more on the significance of Matthew 23:37-39, see below, Chapter Sixteen, "Life From the Dead."

8. Brown, *The Restoration of the Jews*, p. 153.

9. Hans K. LaRondelle, *The Israel of God in Prophecy. Principles of Prophetic Interpretation* (Berrien Springs, MI: Andrews Univ. Press, 1983), comes to the opposite conclusion. According to him, "the New Testament unmistakably *universalizes* Israel's territorial promises…the Middle East focus, or Palestinian restriction, is consistently eliminated in its ecclesiological and apolcalyptic applications….Even in Romans 9-11 Paul does not look for a restored theocracy of national Palestine…" (p. 208, his emphasis). LaRondelle's book represents the official Seventh Day Adventist position which believes that the

Church has become the New Israel, completely replacing natural Israel. Church History Professor Kenneth A. Strand calls this the best book he has seen on the subject, recommending that it be "in the hands of every Christian minister and of all laymen who need to deal with the present-day issues relating to Israel and prophecy" (p. x). This is a recommendation I cannot affirm. For LaRondelle's interpretation of Matthew 23:39, see below, Chapter Sixteen, n. 3.

10. See Gordon J. Wenham, *Genesis 1-15,* WBC (Waco, TX: Word, 1987), p. 332, with special reference to Gerhard Hasel, "The Meaning of the Animal Rite in Gen 15," *Journal for the Study of the Old Testament* 19 (1981), pp. 61-78; for reference to the ceremony of passing through the pieces elsewhere in the Bible, see Jeremiah 34:18.

11. Cf. Romans 11:29 in Today's English Version: "For God does not change his mind about whom he chooses and blesses"; and in the Living Bible: "For God's gifts and his call can never be withdrawn; he will never go back on his promises." Contrast this with the remark of Charles Provan: to say that "God's love for Israel is unconditional...is clearly not the case, unless we say that Scripture contradicts itself." (*The Church Is Israel Now,* p. 3).

In his exhaustive commentary on Romans, James D. G. Dunn notes that, "He who foresees the end from the beginning does not need to tailor his election to the changing circumstances of Israel's belief and unbelief..." Thus, "the call which Israel first received...has never been withdrawn." (*Romans 9-16,* WBC [Waco, TX: Word, 1988], p. 694). That is the meaning of irrevocable! Even Ernst Kasemann, a radical New Testament scholar, saw that "for Paul the church does not simply replace Israel," pointing out that, "The problem of Israel after the flesh cannot be shoved aside if one is not to end up with Marcion." (Marcion was an influential second century spiritual leader who removed the Old Testament from his canon of Scripture!) See Kasemann's *Commentary on Romans* (trans. and ed. by

Geoffrey W. Bromiley, Grand Rapids: Wm. B. Eerdmans, 1980), p. 261. While Kasemann and Dunn, scholars of very different backgrounds, *disagree* on many important points, they *agree* on the permanence of God's covenant with Israel. It is not just dispensationalists who *literally* believe Romans 11:29!

12. Actually, the existence of anti-missionary groups like Jews for Judaism and (in Israel) Yad L'Achim give clear evidence to the fact that Jews *are* being won to faith in Jesus the Messiah. If not, there would be much less for these groups to do! Thank God for the tens of thousands of Jews worldwide who are now walking in Yeshua's light.

13. Referring to God's covenant with Israel, Peter C. Craigie says, "The law of the covenant expresses the love of God and indicates the means by which a man must live to reflect love for God." See *The Book of Deuteronomy*, NICOT (Grand Rapids: Wm. B. Eerdmans, 1976), p. 37. See also Samuel J. Schultz, *The Gospel of Moses* (New York: Harper and Row, 1974).

14. For a representative statement from the Koran, see Sura 2:134-141. According to the Koran, true disciples of Moses and Jesus have always been Muslims, followers of the one true religion. See Abdullah Yusuf Ali, ed. and trans., *The Meaning of the Glorious Qur'an* (Cairo and Beirut: Dar Al-Kitab Al-Masri and Dar Al-Kitab Allubnani, n.d.), Vol. 1, p. 136, n. 392; p. 278, n. 824; and Vol. 2, p. 970, n. 3227.

Chapter Thirteen—Natural Children and God's Children

1. According to T. N. Wright, "Romans 1-8 create the problem to which 9-11 is the solution...1-8 is ultimately incomprehensible without 9-11, and vice versa" (*The Messiah and the People of God* [Ph. D. Dissertation, Univ. of Oxford, 1980], p. 220, quoted in Dunn, *Romans 9-16*, p. 519). Of course, the underlying issue that prompted Paul to write these chapters is, "If the promises came to Israel, and Israel, by and large, did not receive them, does that mean the Word of God failed?"

2. As H. P. Liddon correctly explains in his careful treatment
   of the Greek text: "Of those who are by natural descent Israelites, only a certain number really correspond to the im-
   port of the name"; Liddon then refers to the "restriction of
   the true spiritual Israel to a limited number of born Israelites..." (*Explanatory Analysis of St. Paul's Epistle to the
   Romans* [repr., Minneapolis: James and Klock Christian
   Pub. Co., 1977], pp. 156f.).

3. Although Pastor Steve Schlissel claims that "[Charles]
   Provan has demonstrated, incontrovertibly, that the New
   Testament sets forth the Church as a New Israel" (*Restoration of the Jews,* p. 22, n. 51, referring to *The Church Is Israel Now*), the arguments marshalled by Provan are hardly
   incontrovertible. For example, on pp. 1-43 he lists Scriptures to "demonstrate that the Christian Church is Israel now
   because of the fact that the Old Testament titles and attributes of Israel are applied en masse to the Church in the
   New Testament" (p. 1). But where in the New Testament is
   the Church ever called *Jacob?* Yet *Jacob* was used to refer
   to the people of Israel in the Old Testament more than 140
   times! Would anyone ever think of calling the Church
   Jacob? No! That's because the Church is no more the New
   Israel than it is the New Jacob. For that matter, the Church
   is not the New Yeshurun either. (Yeshurun was used four
   times in the Old Testament as a special title for Israel—*not*
   the Church as a whole.)

   Israel is called God's firstborn son in Exodus 4:22, yet the
   Church in the New Testament is never referred to in this
   way. Why? Because, while Gentile believers are a *new*
   people of God, sharing many of the titles and attributes that
   apply to Israel, they neither *become* nor *displace* the old
   people of God: *physical, national Israel.* All the verses compiled by Provan agree with this conclusion; they do not go
   beyond it.

4. For an excellent study of Galatians 6:16, see S. Lewis Johnson, Jr., "Paul and 'The Israel of God': An Exegetical and Eschatological Case-Study," in Stanley D. Toussaint and Charles H. Dyer, eds., *Essays in Honor of J. Dwight Pentecost* (Chicago: Moody Press, 1986), pp. 181-196. Johnson notes that, "In spite of overwhelming evidence to the contrary, there remains persistent support for the contention that the term *Israel* may refer properly to Gentile believers in the present age" (p. 181). Johnson finds this position to be unbiblical: "If there is an interpretation that totters on a tenuous foundation, it is the view that Paul equates the term 'the Israel of God' with the believing church of Jews and Gentiles....[The] doctrine that the Church of Gentiles and Jews is *the* Israel of God rests on an illusion. It is a classic case of tendentious exegesis" (p. 195).

Although Walter Gutbrodt believes that "the Israel of God" in Galatians 6:16 does, in fact, refer to all believers, he notes that "the expression is in a sense to be put in quotation marks." This is because, with the exception of one or two passages, "Paul does not seem to use [the Greek word] *israel* for the new community of God. For, as we may see from R[om]. 9-11, *he neither could nor would separate the term from those who belong to Israel by descent*" (my emphasis). See his article (with Gerhard von Rad and Karl Georg Kuhn) on "Israel, etc.," in Gerhard Kittel, ed., *Theological Dictionary of the New Testament* (henceforth abbreviated as *TDNT*; trans. by Geoffrey W. Bromiley, Grand Rapids: Wm. B. Eerdmans, 1966), Vol. III, pp. 357-391; I have quoted from p. 388. Remarkably, McKeever finds Galatians 6:16 to be "hard, solid Scriptural evidence" that, according to Paul, the Church—and only the Church—is the Israel of God (*Claim Your Birthright*, p. 106).

5. Cf. Ralph Martin, *James*, p. 9.

6. For Galatians 6:16, cf. the NIV, and see Ronald Y. K. Fung, *The Epistle to the Galatians*, NICNT (Grand Rapids: Wm. B. Eerdmans, 1988), pp. 309-311; for Revelation 7:4, see Robert H. Mounce, *The Book of Revelation*, NICNT (Grand Rapids: Wm. B. Eerdmans, 1977), p. 168f, where he states his views quite forcefully.

7. The other "maybes" (or even "probablys") occur in Revelation 2:9 and 3:9, where reference is made to "those who say they are Jews and are not, but are a synagogue of Satan." According to Mounce, *ibid.*, p. 93, "The Jews who blasphemed...were not real Jews. This should be taken in the sense of Romans 2:28-29.... Regardless of their national descent, they had become by their bitter opposition to the church and its message, a synagogue carrying out the activities of God's supreme adversary, Satan." Of course, as G. R. Beasley-Murray notes, "this is not to be generalized, as though John believed that the whole Jewish nation had become the people of Satan. His description applies to a synagogue which implacably opposed the people of Christ (as the synagogue in Philadelphia, 3:8ff.), and so perverted its nature" (*Revelation*, New Century Bible Commentary [Grand Rapids: Eerdmans, 1983], p. 82).

8. See, e.g., Douglas Moo, *Romans 1-8*, Wycliffe Exegetical Commentary (Chicago: Moody Press, 1991), p. 172, who applies Romans 2:29 to all Christians.

9. Dunn speaks of "the true Jew" in his translation of Romans 2:28; see *Romans 1-8*, WBC (Waco, TX: Word, 1988), p. 119.

10. C. E. B. Cranfield, *The Epistle to the Romans*, ICC (Edinburgh: T & T Clark, 1975), Vol. 1, p. 176. Once again, the statement of Charles Provan is surprising: "...those who are Jews by race only are not Jews at all in the eyes of God" (*The Church Is Israel Now*, unnumbered page before Table of Contents). And how does Provan explain the simple fact

that in *most* cases in the New Testament, the word "Jew" refers to Jews who did *not* follow Jesus—in other words, to "those who are Jews by race only"?

11. Even when the people of Israel did not act like God's children, causing the Scriptures to say, "to their shame they are no longer His children" (Deut. 32:5), God promised that He would bring them back: "The LORD will judge His people and have compassion on His servants *when He sees their strength is gone and no one is left, slave or free*" (Deut. 32:36). Look also in the Book of Hosea: No sooner does God say to Israel, "you are not My people, and I am not your God," than He says, "Yet the Israelites will be like the sand on the seashore, which cannot be measured or counted. In the place where it was said to them, 'You are not My people,' they will be called 'sons of the living God' " (Hos. 1:9-10). No sooner does God say of Israel, "she is not My wife and I am not her husband," than He says, "you will call Me 'my husband'...I will betroth you to Me forever; I will betroth you in righteousness and justice, in love and compassion. I will betroth you in faithfulness, and you will acknowledge the LORD" (Hos. 2:2, 16; 19-20).

12. Of course, people who hold to this view don't believe they are going beyond the meaning of the Word. They would agree with the statement of Gordon D. Fee, a fine New Testament scholar: The understanding that "God's new people are the true Israel of God, who fulfill his promises made to the fathers," is "thoroughing in Paul. See esp. Rom. 2:26-29; 11:17-24; Gal. 3:6-9, 29, 6:16; Phil. 3:3; etc" (*First Corinthians*, p. 444 and n. 14).

13. "As a nation Israel had become apostate, a spiritual harlot in rebellion against her husband. The fearful words of Hebrews 6:4-8 were literally applicable to the covenant nation, which had forfeited its birthright" (David Chilton, *Paradise Restored*, p. 81). And to whom did Israel forfeit its

birthright? Gentile Christian author James McKeever has the answer: "I am an Israelite, and I am very happy to be one" (*Claim Your Birthright,* p. 13). As for the hypothetical man described by McKeever as "Abe Goldstein, who lived in Jerusalem and did not know Christ," the reason Christians would think that he was actually a Jew "is because they really do not believe the Bible..." (*ibid.,* p. 81)!

14. The work of Schlissel and Brown, *Restoration of the Jews,* is a good example of this. (The authors cite many other important Christian thinkers who represent this position.)

15. Reinhold Mayer, in Colin Brown, ed., *New International Dictionary of New Testament Theology* (henceforth abbreviated as *NIDNTT*; Eng. ed., Grand Rapids: Zondervan, 1986), Vol. 2, p. 316.

16. Or, simply, "prayer to God for them" (this is the most likely textual reading). Of course, "for them" means "for the Israelites."

17. See James Dunn, *Romans 9-16,* pp. 659f.

18. During the Holocaust, M.D. Weissmandel, a Polish Jew, appealed for help to the papal ambassador, asking him to intervene on behalf of innocent Jews, especially children. He was told: "There is no innocent blood of Jewish children in the world. All Jewish blood is guilty. You have to die. This is the punishment that has been awaiting you because of that sin" (namely, the crucifixion of Jesus). See Eliezer Berkovits, *Faith After the Holocaust* (New York: Ktav, 1973), p. 19. Berkovits correctly points out that, "Not all Christians felt that way, but many in high offices in the churches did. The deicide accusation through the ages did its murderous work in the Christian subconscious making Christianity, in many cases, an active accomplice in the Nazi crime and, in most cases, 'a tacit party to the barbarities.' " See *ibid.,* pp. 19f.

19. McKeever, *Claim Your Birthright,* p. 229. McKeever is more dogmatic elsewhere. For example, on p. 118 he writes: "After much intense prayer, flat on my face, the Lord clearly spoke to me and said: *This is My truth: the church is Israel. Proclaim My truth and I will bless you.*"

20. Louis DeCaro, *Israel Today,* pp. 108f. In a similar vein, Charles Provan, dealing with Romans 11:17-24, fails to notice that the words "*their own* olive tree" are spoken by Paul with reference to *unbelieving Israelites* who will one day be grafted back in. (See *The Church Is Israel Now,* p. 46. Steve Schlissel, who strongly endorsed Provan's book [above, n. 3], found his treatment of Romans 11 to be "wholly inadequate." See *Restoration of the Jews,* p. 22, n. 51.) According to Paul, unbelieving Israel is still Israel!

Chapter Fourteen—"Thou Shalt Not Steal"

1. See H.H. Ben-Sasson, et al., "Apostasy," *Enc. Jud.,* Vol. 3, cols. 201-215.

2. See Juster and Intrater, *Israel, the Church and the Last Days,* pp. 23-62; and George Ladd, *The Gospel of the Kingdom. Scriptural Studies in the Kingdom of God* (repr., Grand Rapids: Wm. B. Eerdmans, 1988).

3. See Dunn, *Romans 9-16,* pp. 844-853, on these verses.

4. There is no doubt that the subject of Isaiah 54:11-17 is, first and foremost, the city of Jerusalem. See the Aramaic translation (called Targum Jonathan) used in the synagogues in ancient times: "Oh poor humiliated one, the city of whom the peoples say, 'She will not be comforted'..." Franz Delitzsch, who beautifully applies these verses to "the church" (i.e., the people of God), still makes it clear that "Jerusalem is [its] metropolis," stating that Isaiah 54:1ff. is "addressed to Jerusalem." See his *Isaiah,* Vol. 7, Part Two, pp. 348 and 342.

5. See the references to Zion in H. Schultz, "Jerusalem," *NIDNTT*, Vol. 2, pp. 324-329; and Georg Forher and Eduard Lohse, "Zion, Jerusalem, etc.," *TDNT*, Vol. 7, pp. 292-338.

6. This is totally clear from the context of the entire chapter.

7. We are urged in the Book of Psalms to pray for the welfare and peace (*shalom*) of the city of Jerusalem (Ps. 122), the city Jesus wept over (see Chapter Ten, "More Tears") and the city to which He will return (see Chapter Sixteen, "Life From the Dead").

8. See John Bright, *A History of Israel* (Philadelphia: Westminster Press, 1981), pp. 362ff.

9. See Martin Gilbert, *Atlas of Jewish History* (New York: Dorsett Press, 1984), Map 106.

10. See below, Chapter Sixteen, and n. 7.

11. This is the view of authors and teachers like Pike, McKeever, Godwin, DeCaro and Chilton, quoted in the notes to the previous chapters. See the survey of some of their writings (they are all quite dogmatic on this point) in Powledge, *Replacement Theology*, Chapter 1, "Replacement Theology Today," and Appendix D, "Is Replacement Theology Anti-Zionist?"

12. According to present estimates, it is possible that the Russian exodus could almost *double* Israel's Jewish population. For some spiritual insights into the importance of this phenomenal event, see Steve Lightle with Eberhard Muhlan and Katie Fortune, *Exodus II. Let My People Go!* (Eng. ed., Kingwood, TX: Hunter Books, 1983). For Jeremiah 16:14f. and 23:7f. in their original contexts, see the commentaries on Jeremiah by J.A. Thompson, John Bright, William McKane, William L. Holladay and Walter Brueggeman.

Chapter Fifteen—A Diabolical Plan

1. "The very word *Jew* continues to arouse passions as does no other religious or national name." (Prager and Telushkin, *Why the Jews?*, p. 12).

2. See above, Chapter Two, "A Terrible Tragic Past"; Chapter Twelve, n. 3; and Flannery, *Anguish of the Jews*, p. 355 (see the Index under "Deicide accusation").

3. See Flannery, *ibid.*, pp. 7-27; and J.N. Sevenster, *The Roots of Pagan Anti-Semitism* (Leiden: E.J. Brill, 1975).

4. See Prager and Telushkin, *ibid.*, pp. 73f. and 154-157.

5. "However true the 'scapegoat' theory may be in general terms, it does not explain why the Jews rather than some other minority group are picked on, nor does it make clear what they are a scapegoat *for*" (George Orwell, quoted in Gould, *What Did They Think of the Jews?*, p. 472).

6. Cf. the comments of Voltaire, cited below. A recent article entitled "The Bad Nature of the Jews," published in Sydney by the *Australian Chinese Daily*, accused the Jews of being "heartless, rich, cruel, and ruthless warmongers." Tony Wong, the paper's chief administrator, offered an apology, saying "that the article was printed 'inadvertently' " (*Dateline: World Jewry*, June 1991, p. 8). Just think: An *anti-Semitic* article was published in *Australia* for *Chinese* readers!

7. In the words of Edward Flannery, "Antisemitism is the longest and deepest hatred of human history....What other hatred has endured some twenty-three centuries and survived a genocide of 6,000,000 of its victims in its twenty-third century of existence only to find itself still intact and rich in potential for many years of life?" (*Anguish of the Jews*, p. 284).

8. This is the whole argument of Prager and Telushkin in *Why the Jews?* "Throughout their history Jews have regarded Jew-hatred as an inevitable consequence of their Jewishness. Contrary to modern understandings of antisemitism, the age-old Jewish understanding of antisemitism does posit a universal reason for Jew-hatred: Judaism" (p. 21).

9. In Flannery's evaluation, "Prager and Telushkin argue convincingly that Judaism and its positive impact on the Jew is the essential root of all antisemitism. It is an important contribution, but does not sufficiently respect the complexity of the antisemitic reaction since it fails to sound the depths and vagaries of the negative reaction of the antisemite." (*Ibid.*, p. 349, n. 4).

10. Our history is filled with acts of heroism, devotion and sacrifice, with amazing achievements and incredible tenacity; the recent study of Berel Wein, *The Triumph of Survival. A Story of the Jews in the Modern Era (1660-1990)* (Suffern, NY: Shaar Press, 1990), provides ample testimony of this. Still and all, our history has *not* evidenced the promised blessings of the Sinai Covenant.

11. In 1975, Aaron ("Art") Katz attended a Holocaust presentation given by Elie Wiesel in a New Jersey synagogue. Katz, a Jewish believer in Jesus, approached Wiesel at the end of the evening and asked, "To what degree has your study of the Scriptures given you insight into the cause of the Holocaust with which you are identified as the leading Jewish literary figure? I am thinking particularly about the judgment of which God speaks in the concluding chapters in Leviticus and Deuteronomy." Wiesel briefly answered, "I will not consider *that*." See Aaron Katz with Phil Chomak, *Reality. The Hope of Glory* (Pineville, NC: MorningStar Publications, 1990), pp. 77f.

12. See Deuteronomy 5:29 and Isaiah 48:18f.

13. According to Eliezer Berkovits, at the time of the Holocaust, "the overwhelming majority of Jews in Eastern Europe were Torah-observant" (*With God in Hell,* p. 2), and Irving Rosenbaum stated, "It has been estimated that more than half of the millions of Jews caught up in the Holocaust observed the *mitzvot,* the commandments of the Torah, in their daily lives prior to the advent of the Nazis" (*The Holocaust and Halakhah,* p. 1 and p. 157, n. 1). And yet the Holocaust still happened! There are Jewish scholars, however, who would argue differently, pointing out that European Jewry was in a state of spiritual decline.

14. See Luke 19:41-44 (quoted above in Chapter Ten, "More Tears") and then consider the fact that the first hundred years after Jesus' death and resurrection were marked by the destruction of the Temple (in the Jewish uprising against Rome, 66-70 C.E.) and the banishing of all Jews from Jerusalem (after the second uprising against Rome, 132-135 C.E.). The number of Jewish casualties in these wars was astronomical. *If the apostles' proclamation of the risen Messiah had been received, Jewish history would have been very different.*

15. There are parallel examples in the Scriptures: Although God raised up Assyria to judge Israel and Judah, *Assyria went too far* and was herself judged by God (see Isaiah 10:5-19). Less than two centuries later, Babylon was raised up to judge Judah and Jerusalem—Nebuchadnezzar was actually called God's servant (see Jeremiah 27:6)—only to be subsequently judged by God (see Isaiah 47). The nations have always become carried away in their hostility against the Jewish people!

16. Yossel Rakover, quoted by Fackenheim in Talmage, *Disputation and Dialogue,* p. 302 (author's emphasis). See above, Chapter Eleven, n. 11.

17. These were some of Eichmann's last words to his men before the end of the war. See Gabriel Bach, "Adolf Eichmann," *Enc. Jud.,* Vol. 6, col. 520. Alois Brunner, a chief

aide to Eichmann, "told the *Chicago Sun Times* in a 1987 telephone interview from his Damascus home that he regretted nothing and would do it all again. All Jews 'deserved to die because they were the devil's agents and human garbage,' he said" (Davis, *Myths and Facts*, p. 146).

18. Elie Wiesel and Albert H. Friedlander, *The Six Days of Destruction. Meditations toward Hope* (New York/Mahwah: Paulist Press, 1988), pp. 33f.

19. *Ibid.*, p. 34.

20. This occurred September 1, 1942, and is recounted by Ben Edelbaum, an eye-witness (see Gilbert, *The Holocaust*, pp. 440-443). One of the hospital patients taken away to execution that day was Edelbaum's sister, Esther, still hospitalized after the recent birth of her first child. *One of the infants hurled that day from the hospital window to the pavement was Esther's newly born baby girl, the niece of Ben Edelbaum and the first grandchild in the family.* She had not even been named.

21. See the account of N. Hanover, cited in Ben-Sasson, *A History of the Jewish People*, p. 656.

22. In his Preface to the reprint of Hay's *Christian Anti-Semitism*, p. xxi, Flannery refers to "the demonic quality of the phenomenon that turns saints into sadists, savants into muddleheads, and common folk into assasins."

23. Voltaire, quoted in Gould, *ibid.*, pp. 89 and 91. Historian Arthur Hertzberg pointed out that Voltaire "abandoned entirely the religious attack on the Jews as Christ-killers or Christ-rejectors. He proposed a new principle on which to base his hatred of them, their innate character" (quoted in *ibid.*, p. 91).

24. See above, Chapter Two, "A Terrible, Tragic Past."

25. Richard Wagner, quoted in Gould, *ibid.*, p. 196.

26. Arnold Toynbee, quoted in *ibid.*, pp. 453f.

27. Notable anti-Semites of the twentieth century include: Joseph Stalin, whose massive plot against Russia's Jews was stopped only by his death; and Henry Ford, the greatly admired American industrialist whose widely read articles on "the international Jewish conspiracy" were translated into German for distribution by Hitler. (Hitler affectionately called him Heinrich Ford.) It was only after Ford and his paper were convicted of libel that he publicly repudiated these articles.

28. See Hier, Wiesenthal Center letter, p. 1.

29. Raymond Barre, quoted in *Dateline: World Jewry*, January 1991, p. 5.

30. See Prager and Telushkin, *Why the Jews?*, pp. 110-126; Davis, *Myths and Facts*, pp. 283ff. (some of the quotes assembled here do not reflect an exclusively Islamic perpsective); note also the relevant sections of Emmanuel Sivan, *Radical Islam. Medieval Theology and Modern Politics* (New Haven: Yale Univ. Press, 1990).

31. See Juster and Intrater, *Israel, the Church and the Last Days*, pp. 63-141.

Chapter Sixteen—Life From the Dead

1. The Messianic significance of these words is clearly seen in the parallel accounts in the other Gospels: "Blessed is the coming kingdom of our father David!" (Mark 11:10); "Blessed is the king who comes in the name of the Lord!" (Luke 19:38); "Hosanna!...Blessed is the King of Israel!" (John 12:13). See also Hermann L. Strack and Paul Billerbeck, *Kommentar zum Neuen Testament aus Talmud und Midrasch* (Munchen: C.H. Beck, 1922), Vol. 1, p. 850; Joachim Jeremias, *The Eucharistic Words of Jesus* (Eng. trans., Philadelphia: Fortress Press, 1977), pp. 251-261; and

Leslie C. Allen, *Psalms 101-150,* WBC (Waco, TX: Word, 1983), pp. 124f.

2. In the words of W.D. Davies, "the final act of all history rests upon the Jews" ("Paul and the Gentiles: A Suggestion concerning Romans 11:13-24," p. 154, repr. in *Jewish and Pauline Studies* [Philadelphia: Fortress Press, 1984], and quoted in Dunn, *Romans 9-16,* p. 658).

3. For a treatment of Matthew 23:39 that misses the point, see LaRondelle, *The Israel of God in Prophecy,* pp. 160-164. He forgets that Matthew 23:39 goes hand in hand with the future application of Zechariah 12:10: The Jewish people will one day look on the Pierced One, welcoming Him as the coming King. This is *not* "a new way of salvation—'by sight' instead of 'by faith'—[which] goes against the very grain of the eternal gospel of God (see Romans 10:17)" (*ibid.,* p. 162)! Not surprisingly, LaRondelle deals with Matthew 23:39 in his section entitled "Problematic Texts" (pp. 147-169), along with Amos 9:11-12 (as applied in Acts 15:16-18); Isaiah 11:10-12 (Israel's "Second Gathering"); and Luke 21:24 (in the context of the Six Day War of 1967).

4. Commenting on these verses, F.F. Bruce writes: "Let them therefore repent, let them repudiate with abhorrence their acquiesence in the murder of their true Messiah, let them turn back in heart to God, and the salvation and blessing procured by their Messiah's death would be theirs. Their sins would be blotted out...[and not] only would their sins be blotted out; those times of refreshment and joy which the prophets had described as features of the new age would be sent to them by God" (*The Book of Acts,* p. 84).

5. "If the Jewish world ever receives a demonstration of the love that Jesus taught in the Sermon on the Mount, it will have an impact on the Jewish world that will cover a multitude of collective sins by Christians over the centuries" (Shlomo Hizak, *Building or Breaking,* p. 54). Flannery

refers to true repentance of Christian anti-Semitism as "an exorcism of the demons of the past" (*Anguish of the Jews*, p. 3). How these demons need to be driven out!

6. This is important to remember! Some of the authors and teachers I have strongly disagreed with in the previous chapters are committed and sincere believers. As Edward Flannery wrote, authentic Christians "can only rue the fact that Christian antisemitism, while milder today, continues to stain the souls of many Christians" (*Anugish of the Jews*, p. 294).

7. Many Jewish leaders are skeptical about the "unconditionality" of Christian love. What if the Jews (including, of course, the people of Israel) do not immediately follow the Christian script? What if they continue to deny the Messiahship of Jesus? Will the Church *still* love Israel "unconditionally," or will it once again go the way of Chrysostom and Luther?

8. Right now in China, according to *conservative* estimates, 20,000 to 30,000 Chinese are being born again *every day*. (That works out to more than *one million* every six weeks!) Many of these saints have been imprisoned, tortured and even martyred, but that has only served to *increase* the growth of the Chinese church; see Arthur Wallis, *The China Miracle. A Silent Explosion* (Columbia, MO: Cityhill Publishing, 1986). And as the Iron Curtain crumbles, huge crowds of spiritually starved people, from Russia, Ukraine, Romania, Bulgaria and other nations, have come by the tens of thousands to hear the Good News. Yet there is a greater harvest still to come! See Michael L. Brown, *The End of the American Gospel Enterprise* (Shippensburg, PA: Destiny Image, 1989), "The Revival to End All Revivals," pp. 113-116.

9. James Dunn, following Ulrich Wilckens, notes that "not only the extension of the gospel to the Gentiles was

mediated through Israel, but the final act of salvation is also mediated through Israel" (*Romans 9-16,* p. 658). And so, according to Romans 11, this is the "final sequence: fullness of Gentiles (v 25), fullness of Jews (v 12) = reconciliation of the world > the final resurrection" (*ibid.*). Hallelujah!

Bibliographical Supplement

Some of the works cited below are also found in the endnotes. Many books have been cited according to the most recent date of publication; for original date, edition and place of publication, the volumes themselves must be consulted. With rare exception, I have listed works written only in English; however, multi-lingual bibliographies are found in many of the following titles.

Chapter One

The literature on the Holocaust is vast and continues to grow rapidly. Major historical studies include: Lucy S. Dawidowicz, *The War Against the Jews 1933-1945* (New York: Bantam, 1986); Raul Hillberg, *The Destruction of the European Jews*, 3 vols. (New York: Holmes & Meier, 1985); Nora Levin, *The Destruction of European Jewry 1933-1945* (New York: Schocken, 1973); Leni Yallin, *The Holocaust* (New York: Oxford University Press, 1990). Especially rich in eyewitness accounts is: Martin Gilbert, *The Holocaust: A History of the Jews of Europe During the Second World War* (New York: Henry Holt, 1985). For the tragic and moving diary of an entire community, see Alan Adelson and Robert Lapides, eds., *The Lodz Ghetto: Inside a Community Under Siege* (New York: Viking, 1989). An excellent anthology by leading Holocaust authors is:

Albert H. Friedlander, ed., *Out of the Whirlwind: A Reader of Holocaust Literature* (New York: Schocken, 1976). A major pictorial collection is: Yitzhak Arad, *Pictorial History of the Holocaust* (Jerusalem/New York: Yad Vashem/MacMillan, 1991). The authoritative reference work is: Israel Gutman, ed., *Encyclopedia of the Holocaust*, 4 vols. (New York: MacMillan, 1990). See also the works cited at the end of the Supplement to Chapter Four (regarding Jewish piety during the Holocaust), as well to Chapter Seven (regarding the denial of the Holocaust). For a listing of thousands of other studies, see Abraham J. Edelheit and Herschel Edelheit, eds., *Bibliography on Holocaust Literature* (Boulder, CO: Westview Press, 1986); and *idem, Bibliography on Holocaust Literature: Supplement* (Boulder, CO: Westview Press, 1990).

Chapter Two

For general surveys of the history of "Christian" anti-Semitism, see Edward Flannery, *The Anguish of the Jews: Twenty-Three Centuries of Antisemitism* (New York/Mahwah: Paulist Press, 1985); John G. Gager, *The Origins of Anti-Semitism* (Oxford: Oxford Univ. Press, 1983); Malcolm Hay, *The Roots of Christian Anti-Semitism* (New York: Liberty Press, 1981); Jules Isaac, *The Teaching of Contempt: Christian Roots of Anti-Semitism* (New York: Holt, Rinehart, and Winston, 1964); James Parkes, *The Conflict of the Church and the Synagogue: A Study in the Origins of Antisemitism* (New York: Atheneum, 1985); David A. Rausch, *A Legacy of Hatred: Why Christians Must Not Forget the Holocaust* (Grand Rapids: Baker, 1990); Rosemary R. Reuther, *Faith and Fratricide: The Theological Roots of Anti-Semitism* (New York: Seabury, 1974); Samuel Sandmel, *Anti-Semitism in the New Testament?* (Philadelphia: Fortress, 1978); Frank Ephraim Talmage, ed., *Disputation and Dialogue: Readings in the Jewish-Christian Encounter* (New York: Ktav/Anti-Defamation League of B'nai B'rith, 1975); see also the works cited in the Supplements to Chapters Six, Seven and Fifteen. For responses to the charge that the New Testament and/or Christology itself is anti-Semitic, cf. Gregory Baum, *Is the New Testament Anti-Semitic?* (New York: Paulist Press, 1965); Eugene

Fischer, *Faith Without Prejudice: Rebuilding Christian Attitudes Toward Judaism* (New York: Paulist Press, 1977), pp. 54-75; Donald A. Hagner, *The Jewish Reclamation of Jesus: An Analysis and Critique of the Modern Jewish Study of Jesus* (Grand Rapids: Zondervan, 1984), pp. 288-293; T. A. Indinopulos and R. B. Ward, "Is Christology Inherently Anti-Semitic?" *Journal of the American Academy of Religion* 45 (1977), pp. 193-214; Daniel Juster, "Are the Gospels Anti-Semitic?", in *idem* and John Fischer, eds., *The Enduring Paradox: Jewishness and Belief in Jesus* (forthcoming); M. Barth, "Was Paul an anti-Semite?", *Journal of Ecumenical Studies* 5 (1968), pp. 78-104; W. D. Davies, "Paul and the People of Israel," in his *Jewish and Pauline Studies* (Philadelphia: Fortress, 1984), pp. 123-152 (esp. 134-143); Franz Mussner, *Tractate on the Jews: The Significance of Judaism for the Christian Faith* (Philadelphia: Fortress, 1984), pp. 133-153.

Chapter Three

I am not aware of any scholarly books devoted specifically to the general subject of Christian "philo-Semitism." For acts of Christian heroism during the Holocaust, see Philip Friedman, *Their Brother's Keepers* (New York: Crown Publishers, 1957); Mordecai Paltiel, *Path of the Righteous: Gentile Rescuers of Jews During the Holocaust* (Hoboken, NJ: Ktav 1991); Andre Stein, *Quiet Heroes: True Stories of the Rescue of Jews by Christians in Nazi-occupied Holland* (New York: Columbia Univ. Press, 1991); Nechama Tec, *When Light Pierced Darkness: Christian Rescue of Jews in Nazi Occupied Poland* (New York: Oxford Univ. Press, 1986); and the literature cited in Flannery, *Anguish of the Jews* (cited in the Supplement to Chapter Two, above), p. 336, n. 27. For the Corrie ten Boom story, see Corrie ten Boom, with John and Elizabeth Sherrill, *The Hiding Place* (Old Tappan, NJ: Revell, 1971); and Corrie ten Boom, *Prison Letters* (Old Tappan, NJ: Revell, 1975). Note also *Christian History* 32 (Vol. X, No. 4), on Dietrich Bonhoeffer; and cf. Jakob Jocz, *The Jewish People and Jesus Christ After Auschwitz: A Study in the Controversy Between Church and Synagogue* (Grand Rapids: Baker, 1981).

Chapter Four

Many books have been written on Jewish faith and practice, for the general reader as well as for the advanced student. The following represents just a tiny selection. On Jewish thought and practice, see Benjamin Blech, *Understanding Judaism: The Basics of Deed and Creed* (Northvale, NJ: Jason Aronson, 1991); Haim Halevy Donin, *To Be a Jew* (New York: Basic Books, 1991); Louis Jacobs, *Principles of the Jewish Faith* (New York: Basic Books, 1964); Alfred J. Kolatch, *The Jewish Book of Why* (Middle Village, NY: Jonathan David, 1981); cf. also Joseph Telushkin, *Jewish Literacy* (New York: William Morrow and Co., 1991). On the Holy Days, see Abraham P. Bloch, *The Biblical and Historical Background of the Jewish Holy Days* (New York: Ktav, 1978); Irving Greenberg, *The Jewish Way* (New York: Summit Books, 1988); and the anthologies on the major Holy Days by Philip Goodman (Philadelphia: Jewish Publication Society, 1971-). On Jewish customs, see Abraham P. Bloch, *The Biblical and Historical Background of the Jewish Customs and Ceremonies* (New York: Ktav, 1980); Abraham Chill, *The Minhagim: The Customs and Ceremonies of Judaism, Their Origins and Rationale* (New York: Sepher-Hermon Press, 1979). For an introduction to the main bodies of rabbinic literature, see Noah Aminoah and Yosef Nitzan, *Torah: The Oral Tradition* (World Zionist Organization: Department for Torah Education and Culture in the Diaspora, n.d.); Barry W. Holtz, *Back to the Sources: Reading the Classic Jewish Texts* (New York: Summit Books, 1984); *idem, Finding Our Way: Jewish Texts and the Lives We Lead Today* (New York: Schocken, 1990); Jacob Neusner, *Invitation to the Talmud* (San Francisco: Harper & Row, 1984); *idem, Invitation to the Midrash* (San Francisco: Harper & Row, 1989); Adin Steinsaltz, *The Essential Talmud* (New York: Bantam Books, 1976). Useful collections of rabbinic writings and teachings include: A. Cohen, ed., *Everyman's Talmud* (New York: Schocken, 1975); Nathan N. Glatzer, ed., *Hammer on the Rock: A Short Midrash Reader* (New York: Schocken, 1962); C. G. Montefiore and H. Loewe, eds., *A Rabbinic Anthology* (New York: Schocken, 1974). For Jewish piety during the Holocaust, see Eliezer Berkovits, *With God in Hell* (New York: Sanhedrin Press, 1979); Mordechai Eliab, ed., *Ani Ma'amin*, (Hebrew, "I Believe"; Jerusalem: Mosad Harav Kook, 1988); Yaffa Eliach, *Hasidic Tales of the Holocaust* (New York: Vintage, 1988); Ephraim Oshry, *Responsa from the Holocaust* (New York: Judaica Press, 1989, a translation by Y. Leiman of selections from the five volume Hebrew work *Sheilos Utshuvos Mima'amakim* ["Queries and Responses (concerning Jewish practice and Law) from the Depths"]); Irving J. Rosenbaum, *The Holocaust and Halakhah* (New York: Ktav, 1976). For Jewish prayer and worship, see the Supplement to Chapter Eleven.

Chapter Five

In this Supplement are listed books on the Jewish background to the New Testament, the Jewishness of Jesus, the Jewish roots of the Christian faith, and the prophetic significance of Israel's Holy Days. The Supplement to Chapter Eight lists books primarily dealing with Paul's Jewishness, as well as with contemporary Messianic Jewish issues. The following is a small, but representative, sampling of recent literature, including works authored by Protestant, Roman Catholic, Seventh Day Adventist, Messianic Jewish, Orthodox, Conservative and Reform Jewish scholars: James H. Charlesworth, *Jesus Within Judaism* (Garden City: Doubleday, 1988); *idem*, ed., *Jesus' Jewishness* (New York: Crossroad, 1991); E. P. Sanders, *Jesus and Judaism* (Philadelphia: Fortress, 1986); R. T. France and David Wenham, eds., *Gospel Perspectives, Vol. 3: Studies in Midrash and Historiography* (Sheffield: JSOT Press, 1983); Marvin R. Wilson, *Our Father Abraham: Jewish Roots of the Christian Faith* (Grand Rapids: Eerdmans, 1989); Brad H. Young, *Jesus and His Jewish Parables* (New York/Mahwah: Paulist Press, 1989); Terrance Callan, *Forgetting the Root: The Emergence of Christianity from Judaism* (New York/Mahwah: Paulist Press, 1986); Bernard J. Lee, S.M., *The Galilean Jewishness of Jesus: Retrieving the Jewish Origins of Christianity* (New York/Mahwah: Paulist Press, 1988); Val Ambrose McInnes, O.P., ed., *Renewing the Judeo-Christian Wellsprings* (New York: Crossroad, 1987); Jaques

Doukhan, *Drinking At the Sources* (Mountain View, California: Pacific Press, 1981); David H. Stern, *Restoring the Jewishness of the Gospel* (Jerusalem: Jewish New Testament Publications, 1988); Harvey Falk, *Jesus the Pharisee: A New Look at the Jewishness of Jesus* (New York/Mahwah: Paulist Press, 1985); Samuel Tobias Lachs, *A Rabbinic Commentary on the New Testament: The Gospels of Matthew, Mark and Luke* (New York/Hoboken: The Anti-Defamation League/Ktav, 1987); Philip Sigal, *The Halakah of Jesus of Nazareth According to the Gospel of Matthew* (Lanham, MD: University Press of America, 1986); Irving Zeitlin, *Jesus and the Judaism of His Time* (Oxford: Blackwell, 1988). For an evaluation of contemporary Jewish studies on Jesus, as well as for references to the works of I. Abrahams, S. Ben-Chorin, D. Daube, D. Flusser, J. Klausner, P. Lapide, C. G. Montefiore, S. Sandmel, G. Vermes, *et al.*, see Donald Hagner, *The Jewish Reclamation of Jesus* (cited in the Supplement to Chapter Two, above). For the prophetic meaning of the Holy Days, see Victor Buksbazen, *The Gospel in the Feasts of Israel* (Fort Washington, PA: Christian Literature Crusade, 1954); John Fischer, "The Meaning and Importance of the Jewish Holidays," in Sid Roth, *Time is Running Short* (Shippensburg, PA: Destiny Image, 1990), pp. 177-194; Martha Zimmerman, *Celebrate the Feasts* (Minneapolis: Bethany, 1981); Mitch and Zhava Glaser, *The Fall Feasts of Israel* (Chicago: Moody, 1987); cf. also Joseph Good, *Rosh HaShanah and the Messianic Kingdom to Come: A Messianic Jewish Interpretation of the Feast of Trumpets* (Port Arthur, TX: HaTikvah Ministries, 1989); and Daniel Juster, *Revelation: The Passover Key* (Shippensburg, PA: Destiny Image, 1991).

Chapter Six

On contemporary media bias against Israel, as well as common misconceptions on the Palestinian issue, see Yitschak Ben Gad, *Politics, Lies and Videotape. 3,000 Questions and Answers on the Mideast Crisis* (New York: Shapolsky Publishers, 1991); Leonard J. Davis (eds., Eric Rozenmann and Jeff Rubin), *Myths and Facts 1989: A Concise Record of the Israeli-Arab Conflict* (Washington,

DC: Near East Reports, 1988); Stephen Karetzky and Peter Goldman, eds., *The Media's War Against Israel* (New York: Steimatzky-Shapolsky, 1986); Uri Algom, Daniel Dishon, Yoel Cohen, and Arden J. Goldman, "The War in Lebanon," *Encyclopedia Judaica Year Book 1983/5* (Jerusalem: Keter, 1985), cols. 18-67. A useful monthly publication is produced by CAMERA (Committee for Accuracy in Middle East Reporting in America; Boston, MA); the San Francisco based organization, FLAME (Facts and Logic about the Middle East), sponsors ad campaigns in major magazines and newspapers. For some evangelical Christian perspectives on the mid-East crisis, see David Dolan, *Holy War for the Promised Land: Israel's Struggle to Survive in the Muslim Middle East* (Nashville: Thomas Nelson, 1991); George Grant, *The Blood of the Moon* (Brentwood, TN: Wolgemuth & Hyatt, 1991); and M. Basilea Schlink, *Israel at the Heart of World Events: A Perspective on the Middle East Situation Written During the Gulf War* (Darmstadt-Eberstadt, Germany: Evangelical Sisterhood of Mary, 1991). For a balanced assessment of the Palestinian uprising, see Ze'ev Schiff and Ehud Ya'ari, *Intifada* (New York: Simon & Schuster, 1989). For the human dimensions of the Arab-Israeli struggle, see David K. Shipler, *Arab and Jew: Wounded Spirits in a Promised Land* (New York: Penguin Books, 1987); Raphael Patai, *The Seed of Abraham: Jews and Arabs in Contact and Conflict* (New York: Charles Scribner's Sons, 1986); *idem, The Arab Mind* (New York: Charles Scribner's Sons, 1983); *idem, The Jewish Mind* (New York: Charles Scribner's Sons, 1977); cf. also Amos Elon, *The Israelis: Founders and Sons* (New York: Penguin Books, 1981); and Elias Chacour with David Hazard, *Blood Brothers* (Old Tappan, N.J.:Revell, 1984); for strong criticism of Israel from a Palestinian perspective, cf. Naim Stifan Ateek, *Justice and Only Justice: A Palestinian Theology of Liberation* (Maryknoll, NY: Orbis Books, 1989).

Chapter Seven

For general studies of medieval slander against the Jews, see Joshua Trachtenberg, *The Devil and the Jews: The Medieval Conception of the Jew and its Relation to Modern Antisemitism* (New York: Meridian Books, 1961); and James Parkes, *The Jew in the*

Medieval Community (New York: Sepher-Hermon Press, 1976); see also the *Encyclopedia Judaica* articles on "Blood Libel" (by Haim Hillel Ben-Sasson and Yehuda Slutsky), "Desecration of the Host" (by Cecil Roth), "Wandering Jew" (Yvonne Glikson), "Protocols of the Elders of Zion" (Leon Poliakov), "The Dreyfus Affair" (Moshe Catane) and "The 'Doctors' Plot" (Jonathan Frankel), collected in *Anti-Semitism* (Jerusalem: Keter, 1974). For more on the *Protocols*, a work described by Paul F. Boller, Jr. and John George as "one of the most widely circulating forgeries in modern times" (*They Never Said It: A Book of Quotes, Misquotes, and Misleading Attributions* [New York: Oxford Univ. Press, 1989], pp. 106f.), see esp. Norman Cohn, *Warrant for Genocide: The Jewish World Conspiracy and the Protocols of the Elders of Zion* (New York: Harper & Row, 1966); and cf. also Cliff Goldstein, "The Protocols Bug," *Shabbat Shalom,* January-March 1991, pp. 11-13. The "Khazar conversion" theory of Arthur Koestler has been thoroughly refuted by reputable scholars of Jewish history; for a useful summary of Koestler's errors, see John Powledge, *Replacement Theology: The Denial of Covenant?* (M. Div. Thesis, Messiah Biblical Institute and Graduate School of Theology, 1991), "Appendix C: McKeever, Koestler and the Khazars: Questions of Validity and Factuality in Historical Research"; of special note is the French article by Simon Szyszman, "La Question des Khazars: Essai de Mise an Point," *Jewish Quarterly Review* 73 (1982), pp. 189-202. On the pseudo-scholarly denial of the Holocaust, see Lucy S. Dawidowicz, "Lies About the Holocaust," *Commentary* 70/6 (December, 1980), pp. 31-37; *idem, The Holocaust and the Historians* (Cambridge, MA: Harvard Univ. Press, 1981); Israel Gutman, "Holocaust, Denial of," in *Encyclopedia of the Holocaust,* Vol. 2, pp. 681-686, with bibliography of key monographs on p. 686. On slanderous attacks against the Talmud, see the *Encyclopedia Judaica* articles on "Eisenmenger, Johann Andreas" (Vol. 6, cols. 545f.) and "Rohling, August" (Vol. 14, 224); and note also H. L. Strack and G. Stemberger, *Introduction to the Talmud and Midrash* (Edinburgh: T & T Clark, 1991), pp. 241-244, with bibliography on p. 241. See also the works cited in the Supplements to Chapters Six and Fifteen.

Chapter Eight

Basic studies of the Inquisition include: Henry C. Lea, *A History of the Inquisition in Spain*, 4 vols. (New York: Harbor, 1955); Henry A. F. Kamen, *The Spanish Inquisition* (New York: The American Library, 1966); Cecil Roth, *The Spanish Inquisition* (New York: W. W. Norton, 1964); for additional bibliography, see *Encyclopedia Judaica*, Vol. 8, col. 1407; a key work on the "Conversos" is Cecil Roth, *A History of the Marranos* (New York: Schocken, 1974). For the primary sources, see H. Beinart, ed., *Records of the Trials of the Spanish Inquisition in Ciudad Real*, Vols. 1ff. (Leiden: E. J. Brill, 1974-). On contemporary Messianic Jewish issues, interacting also with the earlier work of J. Danielou, H. J. Schoeps, M. Simon, *et al.*, see Daniel Juster, *Jewish Roots: A Foundation of Biblical Theology for Messianic Judaism* (Rockville, MD: Davar, 1986); Michael Schiffman, *Synagogue of the Messiah: Messianic Judaism from the First Century to the Present* (Bay Terrace, NY: Teshuvah Publishing, 1992); David H. Stern, *Messianic Jewish Manifesto* (Jerusalem: Jewish New Testament Publications, 1988); cf. also Arnold G. Fruchtenbaum, *Israelology: The Missing Link in Systematic Theology* (Tustin, CA: Ariel Ministries, 1989); for a historical perspective on "Jewish Christianity" (i.e., Messianic Judaism), cf. Jakob Jocz, *The Jewish People and Jesus Christ: The Relationship Between Church and Synagogue* (Grand Rapids: Baker, 1979); and Ray A. Pritz, *Nazarene Jewish Christianity: From the End of the New Testament Period until Its Disappearance in the Fourth Century* (Jerusalem/Leiden: Magnes/E. J. Brill, 1988). A strong case for the continuation of the seventh day as the Sabbath has been made by Samuel Bacchiocchi, *From Sabbath to Sunday: A Historical Investigation of the Rise of Sunday Observance in Early Christianity* (Rome: The Pontifical Gregorian Univ. Press, 1977); cf. also *idem, Divine Rest for Human Restlessness: A Theological Study of the Good News of the Sabbath for Today* (Berrien Springs, MI: by the author, 1984); for interaction with Bacchiocchi's work, see D. A. Carson, ed., *From Sabbath to Lord's Day: A Biblical, Historical and Theological Investigation* (Grand Rapids: Zondervan, 1982). For a recent Christian study on the importance of the Sabbath (arguing for its biblical transferral to Sunday), see Will Chantry, *Call the Sabbath a Delight* (Carlise, PA: Banner of Truth, 1991). A classic Jewish work on the Sabbath is Abraham Joshua Heschel, *The Sabbath: Its Meaning for Modern Man* (New York: Noonday Press, 1991). Contemporary study on Paul and the Law is voluminous; for a summary of (and interaction with) key recent scholarship, including the writings of W. D. Davies, L. Gaston, E. P. Sanders, H. Räisänen, H. Hübner, *et al.*, see Stephen Westerholm, *Israel's Law and the Church's Faith: Paul and His Recent Interpreters* (Grand Rapids: Eerdmans, 1988); and cf. James D. G. Dunn, *Jesus, Paul, and the Law: Studies in Mark and Galatians* (Louisville, KY: Westminster, 1990). See also the Supplement to Chapter Five.

Chapter Nine

Basic studies of the Crusades include: Hans E. Mayer, *The Crusades* (Oxford: Oxford Univ. Press, 1972); Robert Payne, *The Dream and the Tomb: A History of the Crusades* (New York: Dorset Press, 1984); Jonathan Riley-Smith, *The Crusades: A Short History* (New Haven: Yale Univ. Press, 1990); Steven Runciman, *A History of the Crusades*, 3 vols. (New York: Cambridge Univ. Press, 1952-1954); Kenneth M. Setton, ed., *A History of the Crusades* (Madison: Univ. of Wisconsin Press, 1969); cf. also Salo Wittmayer Baron, *A Social and Religious History of the Jews*, Vol. 4 (New York/Philadelphia: Columbia Univ. Press/The Jewish Publication Society, 1957); Shlomo Eidelberg, *The Jews and the Crusaders: The Hebrew Chronicles of the First and Second Crusades* (Madison: Univ. of Wisconsin Press, 1977); Francesco Gabrieli, ed., *Arab Historians of the Crusades* (New York: Dorset Press, 1989). For further studies, consult the bibliographical works of Hans E. Mayer (*Bibliographie zur Geschichte der Kreuzzüge*; 1960) and Aziz S. Atiya (*The Crusades: Historiography and Bibliography;* 1962).

Chapter Ten

For the intercessory ministry of tears, see Wesley L. Deuwel, *Ablaze for God* (Grand Rapids: Zondervan, 1989), pp. 237-247; and

Leonard Ravenhill, *Revival God's Way* (Minneapolis: Bethany, 1983), pp. 69-74. For classic examples of the power of broken-hearted prayer, see Captain E. G. Carre, ed., *Praying Hyde* (South Plainfield, NJ: Bridge Publishing, 1982); Norman Grubb, *Rees Howells: Intercessor* (Fort Washington, PA: Christian Literature Crusade, n.d.). A powerful call for Christian compassion toward Israel is: M. Basilea Schlink, *Israel, My Chosen People* (Old Tappan, NJ: Revell, 1988); see also *idem, Comfort, Comfort My People* (Darmstadt-Eberstadt, Germany: Evangelical Sisterhood of Mary, 1989); and cf. Andrew Bonar, ed., *Memoir and Remains of Robert Murray M'Cheyne* (Carlisle, PA: Banner of Truth, 1966), pp. 187-198.

Chapter Eleven

Among the many works written on Jewish prayer and worship, the following serve as useful introductions: Haim Halevy Donin, *To Pray as a Jew* (New York: Basic Books, 1980); Evelyn Garfiel, *Service of the Heart: A Guide to the Jewish Prayer Book* (Northvale, NJ: Jason Aronson, 1989); Abraham Millgram, *Jewish Worship* (Philadelphia: Jewish Publication Society, 1971); Elie Munk, *The World of Prayer*, 2 vols. (New York: Feldheim, n.d.); cf. also the various editions of the *Siddur* (Jewish Prayer Book), esp. the *Art Scroll Siddur*, the *Metsudah Siddur* and the editions of the Prayer Book by the Chofetz Chaim, J. H. Hertz, S. R. Hirsch and Philip Birnbaum. On the Eighteen Benedictions, see Avrohom Chaim Feuer, *Shemoneh Esrei: The Amidah/The Eighteen Benedictions* (New York: Mesorah Publications, 1990).

Chapters Twelve, Thirteen, and Fourteen

On the modern State of Israel and the Bible, cf. Arthur W. Kac, *The Rebirth of the State of Israel: Is It of God or of Men?* (Grand Rapids: Baker, 1976); *idem, The Death and Resurrection of Israel: A Message of Hope for a Time of Trouble* (Grand Rapids: Baker, 1976). For a critique of both Dispensational and Covenantal hermeneutics, emphasizing the unity of the Mosaic and New Covenants, see Daniel P. Fuller, *Gospel and Law: Contrast or Continuum?*; for a critique of Replacement (or Fulfillment) Theology, see the M. Div. Thesis of John Powledge (cited in the Supplement to Chapter Seven, above); and, concisely, Keith Parker, "Is the Church the 'New Israel'? A Biblical Analysis of the Teachings of 'Replacement Theology'," in Sid Roth, *Time is Running Short* (cited in the Supplement to Chapter Eight, above), pp. 203-219; cf. also Daniel Juster, in *idem* and Keith Intrater, *Israel, the Church and the Last Days* (Shippensburg, PA: Destiny Image, 1990), pp. 1-102. Concerning the exegesis of Romans 9-11, see esp. the recent commentaries of James D. G. Dunn (Word) and C. E. B. Cranfield (International Critical Commentary).

Chapter Fifteen

For general studies on anti-Semitism, see Paul E. Grosser and Edwin G. Halpern, *Anti-Semitism, Causes and Effects* (New York: Philosophical Library, 1983); Jacob Katz, *From Prejudice to Destruction: Anti-Semitism, 1700-1933* (Cambridge, MA: Harvard Univ. Press, 1980); Gavin A. Langmuir, *Toward a Definition of Antisemitism* (Berkeley: Univ. of California Press, 1990); Bernard Lewis, *Semites and anti-Semites: An Enquiry into Conflict and Prejudice* (New York: W. W. Norton, 1986); Barnet Litvinoff, *The Burning Bush: Anti-Semitism and World History* (New York: E. P. Dutton, 1988); Leon Poliakov, *The History of Anti-Semitism: From the Time of Christ to the Court Jews* (New York: Schocken, 1974); *idem, The History of Anti-Semitism: From Voltaire to Wagner* (New York: Vanguard Press, 1975); Dennis Prager and Joseph Telushkin, *Why the Jews? The Reason for Antisemitism* (New York: Simon & Schuster, 1983); Jean-Paul Sartre, *Anti-Semite and Jew* (New York: Schocken, 1965). Note also the collection of *Encyclopedia Judaica* articles on anti-Semitism (*Anti-Semitism*, cited in the Supplement to Chapter Seven, above), esp. pp. 1-67; and see the works cited in the Supplements to Chapters Two, Six and Seven. Several organizations that provide regular updates on national and international anti-Semitic activity include: the Anti-Defamation League, the Simon Wiesenthal Center, the World Jewish Congress and the American Jewish Congress.

Chapter Sixteen

For Israel and the end-times, see the Supplement to Chapters Twelve through Fourteen, and note Keith Intrater in Juster and Intrater, *Israel, the Church and the Last Days* (cited in the Supplement to Chapters Twelve through Fourteen, above), pp. 103-141; of the many works which express the connection between fervent prayer and revival, see in particular Leonard Ravenhill, *Why Revival Tarries* (Minneapolis: Bethany, 1990); *idem, Revival Praying* (Minneapolis: Bethany, 1989); Mary Stuart Relfe, *The Cure of All Ills* (Montgomery, AL: League of Prayer, 1988); James Alexander Stewart, *Opened Windows: The Church and Revival* (Asheville, NC: Revival Literature, n.d.); Arthur Wallis, *In the Day of Thy Power* (Columbia, MO/Fort Washington, PA: Cityhill Publishing/Christian Literature Crusade, 1990); cf. also James Edwin Orr, *The Event of the Century: The 1857-1858 Awakening* (Richard Owen Roberts, ed.; Wheaton, IL: International Awakening Press, 1989); Charles G. Finney, *Revival Lectures* (Old Tappan, NJ: Revell, n.d.); and see the Supplement to Chapter Ten.

As of the fifth printing, *Our Hands Are Stained With Blood* has been translated into Finnish, Norwegian, Swedish, Dutch, Russian, Korean, Hungarian, Romanian, and Japanese, with Spanish, Italian and other translations in progress.

ICN Ministries has prepared a complete resource catalog of materials by Dr. Michael L. Brown. Included in this catalog are books, audiotapes, videotapes, and self-study courses dealing with:

- Repentance and Revival
- Spiritual Life
- Prayer and Intercession
- Holiness
- Prophetic Ministry
- Divine Healing
- The Church and the Jewish People
- Answering Jewish Objections to Jesus
- Debate and Dialog with Rabbis and Anti-Missionaries

To request our resource catalog, write, call, or fax to:

ICN Ministries
P.O. Box 36157
Phone: (850) 458-6424
FAX: (850) 458-1828
E-mail: RevivalNow@msn.com

In-Depth Self-Study Courses!

Choose from three courses specially prepared by Dr. Michael L. Brown.

Answering Jewish Objections to Jesus. This 12-tape series asks hard questions and provides solid, sound and scholarly answers. Ideal for all those involved in Jewish outreach and witnessing. Also excellent for those who have been confused by the anti-missionaries. The course comes with study guide and texts. (Dr. Brown's in-depth book on the subject of answering Jewish objections to Jesus will be available in the spring of 1997.)

The Messiah in Jewish Tradition. Learn the many, varied Jewish beliefs about the Messiah, from the Dead Sea Scrolls to the Talmud, from the Bible to Jewish mysticism. A fascinating, firsthand encounter with the ancient and medieval writings. Twelve tapes with textbook and study guide.

I Am the Lord Your Healer. This in-depth, faith-building teaching will help lay solid foundations of the Word in your life. Based on a careful study of the Hebrew and Greek, this comprehensive and practical course can easily be understood by any interested believer. Sixteen tapes, a study guide and Dr. Brown's full-length study *Israel's Divine Healer* are included.

Available through ICN Ministries, P.O. Box 36157, Pensacola, FL 32506; call (850) 458-6424, fax (850) 458-1828, or E-mail: RevivalNow@msn.com.